NOTHING BUT THE TRUTH

THE JOURNEY TO MEETING, AND MASTERING LIFE LESSONS FROM SOME OF INDIA'S MOST POWERFUL PEOPLE

RISHABH SHAH

An imprint of
Srishti Publishers & Distributors

Srishti Publishers & Distributors
A unit of AJR Publishing LLP
212A, Peacock Lane
Shahpur Jat, New Delhi – 110 049

editorial@srishtipublishers.com

First published by Bold,
an imprint of Srishti Publishers & Distributors in 2023

10 9 8 7 6 5 4 3 :

This is a work of non-fiction. All accounts narrated in this book are real life accounts as experienced by the author. It is the author's perspective on how the situations occurred. The views expressed in the book are the author's own and are not intended to hurt the sentiments of any individual, community, sect or religion.

Printed and bound in India

Advance Praise

I have known Rishabh for nearly a decade. I have seen him build IIMUN from scratch into one of the premier student organisations in India, rooted in our culture, and yet, imbibing lessons from the West as well. A young man who could do so much so quickly, must have a lot to teach us. This book gives insights from those that he learned from. Essentially, this book will help us learn from the best of the best, via a brilliant young man like Rishabh, who has shown how to implement those lessons. Read it, learn the lessons, find success and happiness in your life.

– **AMISH TRIPATHI**
Bestselling author, Diplomat

"Take up an idea, devote yourself, struggle in patience and the sun will rise." – Swami Vivekananda.

This quote could not hold truer for Rishabh Shah. A millennial gentleman with a fire in his belly, I have seen an insatiable zeal and conviction in him to make a difference to the world around him.

A multi-faceted individual, he led India's International Movement to Unite Nations (IIMUN), the world's largest youth-run organisation through his late teens and his twenties. This speaks volumes of his entrepreneurial acumen and leadership capabilities.

In this no holds barred book titled Nothing but the Truth *Rishabh highlights the findings based on his personal interface with very successful people in varied fields and brings out their unseen side in a fresh and enticing approach. This book will serve as an inspiration for future generations.*

I wish Rishabh the "Author" roaring success in all that he aspires. May he carry his never say never attitude with aplomb everywhere he goes!

– **AJAY PIRAMAL**
Chairman, Piramal Enterprises Limited

IIMUN has been around for a decade!
Rishab Shah, I'd like to say, "Well played!"
Without hesitation it must be stated
Your sacrifice is appreciated.
What goes around, comes around.
This philosophy is very sound.
While you served you also learned.
Useful life lessons you have earned!
Now with "Nothing but the Truth"
Your readers also learn, forsooth!
Powerful people came your way.
You learnt from them, how to play,
How to seek an interview,
Register learnings that are new
And finding knowledge that's really sound
But unfortunately rarely found,
No matter how hard one looks
In academia or in books.
Although it isn't very wise
There are constant attempts to polarise.
Where echo chambers resound
Balanced views are rarely found
Deep learning can be applied

From politicians across the divide.
We often see the outward face
But many interactions can then place
The person in a different light.
Pappus can be astute and bright.
Personalities from sports and arts
Appeal to our minds and hearts.
The more we learn, the more we know.
Our horizons expand and grow!
This book is an exciting ride.
If the learnings from this book are tried
And different thoughts are all applied
Our youth together can provide
A successful nation that's unified
With its influence spreading far and wide!

– **NADIR GODREJ**
Chairman and MD, Godrej Industries

I have always believed that there is something to learn from everybody. And that is something that this book depicts very well. Having been closely associated with the organisation I.I.M.U.N., I have seen this in action. The youthful energy of the student organizers is palpable and whether it is them or the participants – the young India that I.I.M.U.N. represents is ready to absorb the best out of everyone!

What impresses me the most is how Rishabh has been able to respectfully lay bare the pluses and frailties of some of India's modern greats. Truth can also be sweet. His journey to meeting them is as exciting as the many encounters that he has had with them.

Drawing leadership and life lessons from these stalwarts, his extrapolation of those learnings and how to tackle day-to-day gremlins, makes this a self help book with a difference! In his original self deprecating but insightful commentary, this is a compelling read for both young and old.

– **BOMAN IRANI**
Actor

This book is dedicated to ...

A set of teenagers who did not know what they were doing, and adolescents who got together because of the lack of opportunity to do anything else. They did not have anything to show for, anything to stand for, but a dream which wasn't even fully formed.

To my first team at India's International Movement to Unite Nations.

After all, the most difficult step is the first step in life.

And it is equally difficult to keep it going. Here's to the thousands of teenagers that have followed thereafter; who have prioritised, believed and made possible not just this book, but created a place that some refer to as the school of schools, others the university of universities, and I refer to as home.

I dedicate the book and all proceeds from it to the organisation.

I would also like to thank my parents for having the patience and bearing with me for over twelve years as I relentlessly pursued a dream which helped me open closed doors and learn things which couldn't have been imparted in any B School.

Table of Contents

Foreword .... **xi**

Introduction **1**

Part I: Public Service **7**

Chapter One: Nagpur Ke Santre
with Mohan Bhagwat **9**

Chapter Two: Pappu Ki Pariksha
with Rahul Gandhi **28**

Chapter Three: The Cost of Truth
with Dr. Subramanian Swamy **47**

Chapter Four: A Presidential Address
with Late Fomer President Pranab Mukherjee .. **67**

Chapter Five: Boarding The Payyoli Express
with PT Usha **86**

Part II: Other Fields **107**

Chapter Six: A Man Of Honour
with Late Gen Bipin Rawat **109**

Chapter Seven: How Money Moves
with Deepak Parekh **130**

Chapter Eight: Finding Your Swadharma
with Karan Johar..**148**

Chapter Nine: Striking a Chord
with A.R. Rahman..**168**

Chapter Ten: A Broken Promise
with Syed Akbaruddin..**186**

Backward..**209**

Foreword

I met Rishabh (and his excellent team at the I.I.M.U.N.) for the first time when he was a student and running a large-scale Model United Nations event in Mumbai. I addressed it and was impressed, both by his vision and his drawing power – to attract an impressive roster of speakers and a huge audience – as well as undoubted organizational ability to pull such a large event together while still a student himself.

Having since then seen at close quarters Rishabh's sense of enterprise at building I.I.M.U.N. and his own performance from the ground up over a decade now, I write this foreword with the utmost pleasure. He has converted I.I.M.U.N. from a Model United Nations forum into a Movement to Unite Nations, and in doing so has built up a huge global network of volunteers, participants and alumni, united across nations by a common faith in international co-operation and motivated by the conviction that they can make a difference.

Since the moment I met him, I knew that his is a refreshing and much needed voice in our dwindling discourse. His own credibility has been acquired by dint of hard work and by proof of performance. Rishabh did not come to me through *sifaarish,* the colloquial term for personal recommendation by someone higher-up. If today he has a wide roster of eminent figures across India willing to speak for him, it is only because he has directly impressed every one of us.

Rishabh's innovative approach to leadership and intrinsic willingness to learn – itself the hallmark of a leader – comes out beautifully in *Nothing but the Truth*, as he takes readers on a journey through the lives of some very prominent and influential people, with him as our inimitable guide.

Since my days at St. Stephen's College, in my writing, during my United Nations career, and all the way through to my political avatar, I have publicly vouched for the importance of learning eclectically, across disciplines and spheres of life. That precisely is the thrust of Rishabh's thinking. In his book, one encounters figures as diverse as Mohan Bhagwat, Rahul Gandhi, Karan Johar, A.R. Rahman, and many more voices of brilliant people who have stood out in a variety of different fields. Infused with the effortless charm and wit of Rishabh's own insights, this isn't merely a description of Rishabh's own acquaintance with these people, but a deeper interrogation into the lessons he has imbibed from them. Notably, he does not restrict his lessons to the people themselves, but incorporates how the teams managing these leaders exhibit skills that all of us can learn from.

To my mind, the significance of Rishabh's contribution lies in the destruction of the godlike stereotypes we tend to conjure of so-called celebrities and popular leaders. To us, they stand aloof, a class apart – an almost superhuman category. As I learned during my own encounters with global leaders and international celebrities during my years at the UN, the truth is that, not only are they very human, fallible and replete with their own quirks and eccentricities, but they are also often quite willing to be viewed as such, if given the space to do so on their terms. Rishabh's dynamic and highly readable voice does justice to this human element of the well-known personalities he has chosen. Perhaps even more important, he has achieved a remarkable feat by showing that the exposition of these often embarrassing traits can be done in a positive light and in a mature manner. In today's polarised times, Rishabh's writing is a much-needed whiff of fresh air.

Self-help books are aplenty, but what a lot of them lack is a personal touch. Rishabh stands out by bringing his individual character to the pages of this book. The way he weaves lessons of leadership and management into a very practical understanding of succeeding in the world is testament to the clarity of his insight. Anyone can, perhaps, express what they have learned from someone else. But putting that in the context of the obstacles the world throws in one's path as one seeks to operationalise those learnings, is a laudable achievement.

I am pleased to say, without even a smidgen of hesitation, that fellow readers who pick up this book will not be disappointed. In fact, behind these pages, you are in for a wonderful tour through Rishabh's world, peopled by some ingenious, persevering and (not to forget!) famous inhabitants, complete with young Rishabh's very original voice. Happy reading, and happy learning!

Dr Shashi Tharoor
Member of Parliament
June 2022

Introduction

I come from a generation where instant gratification is fed into our system. An Instagram reel or YouTube short or sometimes even a Tinder date are swiped over in ten seconds; at best, all three stay put for sixty seconds. The number of likes on a post and views on a video determine our Happiness Quotient. Followers on social media dictate how popular you are and how big of an 'influencer' you are.

There is no denying that we're living in a fast-paced world with an overdose of content. In an age of podcasts, to want to pen down my thoughts and that too in a traditional set up with a publisher, was considered by many as an archaic move. But the fact that you have picked up the book is an indication that our breed is not yet dead.

Talking about breeds and bandwagon effects – Ask yourself, how we or how many of our friends, peers or colleagues only seek inspiration from those who echo our beliefs and systems? We often venerate those who we like, put them on a pedestal and condescend anyone who says anything against them. Today, in an increasingly polarized world, it is important to remember the middle path. A Sanskrit Subhashita comes to mind:

अमन्त्रमक्षरं नास्ति नास्ति मूलमनौषधम् ।
अयोग्यः पुरुषो नास्ति योजकस्तत्र दुर्लभः ॥

There is no word without meaning. There is no root without medicinal power.

There is no person who is incompetent or unsuitable. But we see many people as such. And we blame them. There is usually scarcity of the right teacher.

I have been fortunate at a young age to be able to sit across and implicitly learn from people with very different belief systems, without any references to reach them.

And whilst everyone can teach you something, I have tried to narrate stories of those who have profoundly impacted me. Another caveat – I talk about those who I have met on multiple occasions and therefore are people that I can vouch for.

The real influencers of our country are not those who are trending on social media platforms, but the ones who are making things move across the country.

Think business and you will realise that Ratan Tata or Mukesh Ambani are bigger than any unicorn founder.

Think politics and you will understand that the real power centre of the Congress Party lies with the Gandhi family, and the BJP is influenced by those in Nagpur.

Talk of Bollywood and you will see the Johars and Chopras continuing to determine whose value increases or decreases across small and big screens alike.

These people move in restricted circles and access to them is only for a privileged few. Yes, if you come from an incredibly famous, wealthy or powerful family, then perhaps the doors to some of these people may open faster. But in most cases, they live in isolated silos far from the reach of the common man. Ironically, they are the ones who determine the future of every *aam aadmi*.

Wouldn't you like to know how these people lead their lives?

What makes the rich richer?

How less than 1 percent of the country continue to control 40 percent of our nation's wealth?

How only around twenty political families have governed India since 1947?

What did they do to ensure that generations to come enjoy this lasting legacy?

What are the leadership mantras and life laws that govern their existence?

Unfortunately for us, the gremlin, we are privy only to those things that are carefully curated and put in front of us. The image crafted by media houses is often something that the powerful want us to see. Or in some cases what the media wants us to see, based on their own business interests. They create images to make these people look likable, relatable and someone we tirelessly aspire to be.

Nevertheless, it isn't often for the mighty few to accept or train someone who comes purely on merit. In fact, if you ask me, getting in touch with them is the hardest bit. There are so many gatekeepers, that in Karan Johar's case, it took me almost a decade to just get in touch with the man. Therefore, how to break these many layers of bureaucracy that surround these people is a life hack in itself.

After all, your network is your net worth!

In my experience, building your network isn't a game of valuation; it's more about value creation!

When I started off, as a young millennial born in the 1990s, most of these names were people that I saw on television or read about in the papers. I didn't have access to these people and no family lineage was readily available. At least, none which I would accept. In a land where everything works on references or *sifaarish,* none can or have been used.

In this book, get ready to read about the ordeals of an ordinary boy as he tries to meet some of his role models and others, who necessarily weren't his first choice people.

Each chapter works like a map to showcase how I have cracked them open. How and why did Karan Johar respond after a decade? Why did PT Usha entertain someone who can barely run to save his life? What made India's first Chief of Defense Staff drop us to the end of the corridor each time he met us? And why did A.R. Rahman join the Board of an organisation that has little/ no public presence and no eminent personality behind it?

If you finish the book and manage to tolerate my sense of humour, you may even be able to find N number of novel approaches to reach out to those you dream of meeting or working with.

Through this book, I will also show you how these powerful people really are!

Is Rahul Gandhi really a Pappu or a Tapasvee?

Is RSS a Hindu militant organisation that wants to convert the country into a Hindu state?

Would Pranab Mukherjee really have made a better Prime Minister than Manmohan Singh?

Where does Subramaniam Swamy get the muscle to unequivocally call out Sonia Gandhi and Narendra Modi?

What is the cost of truth? I hope it doesn't cost me too much. :-p But for you, by the end of book, you will discover the humane or the not-so-tolerable side of many of these stalwarts.

However, the most important aspect of the book is what leadership and life lessons I picked up on the way, from some of India's most powerful people. I saw Deepak Parekh give a masterclass on why the value of goodwill matters more than a good will. He did this by raising tens of crores in a few minutes. How it taught me that whales in oceans are actually very different from sharks in tanks. Through this book you will discover what I learnt from them (in the process, from their teams and the paraphernalia around them), and what I learnt from *my* team while building the organization – India's International Movement to Unite Nations (I.I.M.U.N.). You'll be surprised at how much your peers and juniors can teach you.

Get ready to read real life stories of resilience, grit and unending perseverance. Imbibe the qualities and traits that make India's most powerful stand out, and I am certain that you will have a better life and greater leadership capabilities.

As Socrates said-

"Smart people learn from everything and everyone,

Average people learn from their experiences,

Stupid people already have all the answers."

I used to fall into the third category, but thanks to my team, I have moved up into the second one. I am certain all you smart people will make the most of this book.

Until we meet in person! Opening the doors!

Part I: Public Service

The world of politics and social work

Part I

Public Service

Chapter One

Nagpur Ke Santre With *Mohan Bhagwat*

Since 2014, India has been governed by a ruling coalition of those who subscribe to the ideology of the Rashtriya Swayamsevak Sangh, or as it popularly referred to as – the RSS. Now, the Bharatiya Janata Party (BJP) may or may not accept its affiliation with its parent body, but let me clear it out for all of you. After the first ban on the RSS was lifted in 1949, there was a long deliberation on whether they would turn political. After all, none of the political parties had supported them when they were banned. Eventually, it was decided that they would not contest themselves, but would not stop members from starting a political party.

And so, Dr Syama Prasad Mukherjee[1] founded the Bharatiya Jana Sangh in 1951 with a few other volunteers. Later, it was merged with the Janata Party. This party first came into power in 1977 with former full time RSS volunteers (*pracharaks*) Atal Bihari Vajpayee and L.K. Advani holding ministerial positions in the Centre. In 1980, the same members left the Jana Sangh to form what is now the BJP.

1 (1901-1953), An Indian politician, academician and barrister.

Despite its vehement denial of involvement in day to day affairs, there is undeniable tracing that RSS over the years has continued to supply manpower to the BJP, its offices used for 'nation building' and its volunteers have then occupied powerful positions, including that of the Prime Minister of India.

RSS maintains that it is not connected to the BJP, though most political analysts say that the real, on-ground support of the BJP is the RSS. With 60,000+ centres or *shakhas*, over 200,000+ active projects and with lakhs of volunteers, the implicit truth is well-known to any ordinary person who follows politics.

A close family friend who worked for years in the BJP coined them as a Hindu nationalist paramilitary volunteer organisation. The paramilitary part always scared me, and I will talk about it later in the chapter.

But for me, I have also seen them as the tree whose branches grew and became the very puissant Sangh Parivar.

An organisation that has penetrated all sections of society with the common aim of building one strong Hindu Rashtra. The aim of spreading the message of 'nation first' to every last citizen.

Therefore, in 2014, when former pracharak of the RSS, Narendra Modi became Prime Minister, people gave the real credit to the RSS. Without a doubt, at that juncture, people mentioned that the power centre was the headquarters of the RSS.

The orange city of Nagpur gained prominence overnight. Sarsanghchalak or head of the RSS was deemed the Prime Minister behind the Prime Minister. India's most powerful man was the very sought after Mohan Bhagwat!

As an organisation, I.I.M.U.N. has always endeavoured to build leaders whose heart beats for India. Whether it is the student volunteers, or the participants at the 220+ annual concourses that the organisation conducts in as many cities, the aim is singular. But what is also undisputed is the fact that all of these student volunteers and participants have political opinions. In a democracy as vibrant as India, the views are multifarious, as they should be.

I too have my opinions. But having been in-charge of the organisation for over a decade, it wasn't advisable for me to express it. But today I can!

I am not one to bifurcate on the basis of religion, caste, creed or nationality. After all, the very tenants of our scriptures talk about the concept of *Vasudhaiva Kutumabakam* or the world being one global village. But the fact that one's identity is defined by the country one is from is an inescapable reality.

Therefore, whether it be having students wear Indian clothes, eat Indian vegetarian food, practice yoga in the morning or simulate Indian councils for debate, my idea of shedding the cloak of western mindset and embracing India was something very similar to the RSS.

In Gen Z language, now you can understand why we were 'vibing'.

Even before the BJP came into power, we were accused of being sympathetic to this ideology. With many people calling us Sanghis, I often wondered what was similar between us. Honestly, not many books gave an understating to what the real RSS was; more so, how and why did they run such a large network of volunteers.

To quench this thirst of curiosity, in early 2015, I first wrote to the office of the RSS Chief, Mohan Bhagwat. As you will notice in most chapters that follow, there was no revert. People in the right wing don't immediately respond, even if your surname has a Shah in it. Or perhaps they saw through it that we may share some processes, but were centrists in approach. Or what is the most likely one – they didn't take us very seriously. I mean, nor did we. It's best to keep it that way.

In my then immediate team called the Core Council that runs I.I.M.U.N., there was one political enthusiast – some would just call him a Modi bhakt at that time – Priyank Vasani. After many failed attempts, I thought RSS wouldn't understand my language and asked him to give it a shot.

He relentlessly pursued the organization. Finally, in early 2016, he was able to get a meeting time fixed with a pracharak called Sunil Deshpande.

I was mighty impressed. I knew how tough it was to get through to this organisation. I had tried and failed.

That just reinforced the important lesson that young people are the only ones that can do the impossible. The wiser you get, the more pragmatic you become. So, whenever someone gives you an impossible target, involve someone who is a teenager or in their twenties. You'll see how they break the word into I-am-possible.

And if you are in that age bracket, I recommend you to build yourself – learn something new every day, meet as many people as you can, travel and keep cracking the paradoxical tasks, or simply join

I.I.M.U.N. I *had* to plug it in; after all, this is the organisation because of which I am writing this book!

When I first saw him, he reminded me of a middle-aged Maharashtrian uncle with a white moustache, abundant white hair, average height, wheatish complexion, lean figure, carrying a sling bag and wearing an off white kurta-pyjama.

Unlike most first interactions which take place at a neutral location like a coffee shop or an office premises, he told us that he would like to come and meet us at *my* house.

It was only later that I realized that this is a normal practice. They want to know an individual and his ecosystem inside out. After all, one can keep up appearances only outside of home. Home is home.

A masterstroke.

Starting out, at I.I.M.U.N. we used to do the same thing, though that was more out of the fact that one couldn't conduct meetings in coffee shops on college funds.

"*Toh kaise ho* Rishabh *bhai*," Sunil ji asked, sipping his sugar free tea on a bright sunny Sunday morning.

I must mention here that Hindi has never been my strong suit. I studied it only as a third language after English and Gujarati. And once in school I wrote an entire Hindi paper in Gujarati and added lines on top of it. Luckily, my teachers didn't read much.

As Priyank and I explained in meticulous fashion, he was eagerly listening to us narrate in half English-half Hindi the reason behind I.I.M.U.N. He let us talk and even when there were awkward silences, he let us take the lead. And when we questioned him, monosyllables were all we got before the spotlight came back on us. The only time he let out a smile was when I said, "We need to help kids like me rediscover India, so that we have more Modi jis and less people like me."

Priyank and I were perplexed by this very strange meeting.

Often, I have observed that the best communicators weren't people such as me who talk too much, but those who talk little.

Silence will always be broken, especially by the one who is nervous and wants to get done with the meeting – a thumb rule few management books taught me.

When you find yourself in such a situation, perhaps try this – remain silent when you have nothing important to say. The person you are talking to will let out more than needed. This has helped me many times in life.

I only wish I knew how to play it cool in front of one of the prettiest girls in school who I had a crush on, or just implement it when I met her again after very many years!

Sometimes we know what to do, but it just doesn't happen, does it?

Post that rendezvous, we followed up with Sunil ji many a time, but to no avail.

And then, out of the blue, a few months later, Sunil ji called Priyank and invited us to the Mumbai headquarters of the RSS.

I realised that the RSS is like a tortoise – they move very slowly, but they surely knew how to win the race. They had ensured that we were nothing but naive, moldable kids before letting us in. On the D Day, we reached a dilapidated building in a blue-collared neighborhood.

For an organisation that had one of its own pracharaks as the Prime Minister, I had presumed it'd be more *a la grande*.

If we hadn't been told this was their Mumbai HQ, we would've never found it.

It's rightly said, "Simplicity is the greatest form of sophistication."

Hygienic, basic and well-maintained were adjectives one could use to describe the floors on which they were located. Each room had a meeting room, an attached bedroom with one/ two charpoys to sleep on, and a bathroom. I soon gathered that this was the pattern for all their premises.

In Gen Z language: Was it aesthetically okay? Definitely not! But it got the job done. And considering what they were setting out to do, this was just about perfect!

As Sunil ji explained the life of a pracharak, I realized how tough it could be. It meant no family, being completely celibate (which in his opinion meant no tension) and without any bank balance. The RSS provides for daily commute and in return pracharaks had to devote their entire life to the organisation.

An impossible task, I thought! To ask teenagers to make sacrifices on their social life to pursue their own dreams is a herculean task, leave alone work towards a common goal that put the nation first.

I knew first hand that recruiting a hundred students and training them was a task in itself, and these people were managing millions. The big question was – *how*?

Then came the offer we were hoping he'd make – to meet Mohan Bhagwat. And as Priyank excitedly got up assuming he was down the hall, Sunil ji let out a laugh and said, "Mohan ji *thodi yahaan hain.*" He was not there at that time.

I remember it was mid-year when the two of us went to taste Nagpur *ke santre* (oranges) for the first time. The nervous palpitation was visible on our faces. After all, we were meeting Mohan Bhagwat. To top it all, his Z+ security apparatus only made us even more fidgety. A good performance would ensure strong relations with the RSS and BJP, and a flop show meant we'd be forgotten forever. No pressure, of course!

I would realise much later that neither of this was true. I overhype and read too much into situations.

Unusual for a man with such security apparatus, a small ground with children playing cricket led us to the house which played home to many senior and retired pracharaks, along with the RSS Chief. There was even a small private museum in the same place. As is the custom of them coming home, he had reciprocally invited us to his residence.

As we sat in his waiting room, we noticed a big map of Akhand Bharat plastered behind us, which included Afghanistan, Pakistan, Bhutan, Nepal, Tibet, Bangladesh, Myanmar and Sri Lanka – all painted saffron.

Sunil ji mentioned, "*Aap bahut bhagyashali ho. Ghar pe Bahut kam logon ko milte hain Sarsanghchalak ji.*" Apparently we were among a select few who Mohan Bhagwat had agreed to meet at home.

With the map and the statement, I didn't know whether to be grateful or run for my life. I nervously smiled.

And in that split second, the conspiracy theories of the RSS having religious conversion units, having played a role in assassinating Mahatma Gandhi – all flashed before me.

Before I could excuse myself out, we were taken to a small seating area just outside his bedroom. Typical of the way RSS quarters were made. Nothing fancy – four sofas, a couple of books and some coffee tables.

And then he arrived! Smiling at us was a man five feet six inches tall, a bald head with some white hair on the sides, a thick white moustache and a developing paunch, and of course, the quintessential off white kurta pyjama. At first glance, one wouldn't classify him as India's most powerful man. You could easily mistake him for that one far off relative who loves to talk.

There are some people who exude power as soon as they walk into a room. But the most powerful people are the ones that seem very ordinary. Mohan Bhagwat fell into the second category. Priyank was quick to touch his feet and I folded my hands in a namaste.

"*Mere pura naam* Rishabh Sanjay Shah *hain. Yeh* RSS *ko* RSS *ko milne ka mauka diya, uska bahut* thank you."

Now re-read that line with a British accent.

And he responded in English, "The British have left, but they seem to have left your friend Shashi Tharoor and you behind!"

As Sunil ji and Priyank burst out laughing, the ice was broken. I realised the man had done his homework.

Now please understand, here were two kids with little real world impact and this man had comprehensively read up about us. He knew where we lived, what we did – everything. Just went on to show how seriously he took every meeting.

I realized much later in life how important this quality is, and why it sets them apart. To have every last piece of information before commenting is crucial in every walk of life, whether it is about the girl you are proposing to or the business deal you are about to make.

The conversation was interlaced with interesting anecdotes and often ventured towards how India is the only country that can unite the world.

Though I must confess, the map didn't necessarily add up to the conversations we were having.

I then veered to the topic of inviting him to an I.I.M.U.N. concourse. And he readily consented.

"Par aapko bhashan Hindi mein dena padega aur mein 2016 mein aaunga."

Bewildered, of course because Hindi, but also the timeline. I looked at Sunil ji, who removed his calendar and I was shocked to see all dates till March 2016 filled.

This is something that Priyank and I discussed at length and used this example for many years.

Most of us don't know what we are doing the next day, and this man knew what he wanted to do for every single day for the next year.

It was un-freakin-believable!

I've often encountered that the most methodological and well-planned people go far. Even what society perceives as a stroke of genius requires a lot of planning.

After all, my namesake in cricket Rishabh Pant's audacious shot making is also a result of a lot of practice.

Do you remember? Up until we used to get a weekly calendar from school, life was systematic. Unfortunately, we don't create a calendar for our life.

And if you do, my bad, you are already many steps ahead of me.

His last words which I will never forget were, *"Aap bhi desh ke liye man-making kar rahe ho, aur hum bhi. Dhyan rahe dusro ko aage karna hain, khud ko nahi, issi mein Bharat akhand hoga. Milke achhaa laga ji."*

He had drawn a parallel; our organization in its own infinitesimal manner was also aiming to mould young people and create leaders. He advised us to encourage others to take the lead. Back then, I didn't understand the gravitas of the statement. But somehow it makes sense now. In this race of life, everyone is wanting to become someone. I've often been tempted to do things for myself, only to go back to that statement and realise that one isn't running the race in the first place. This has become a life advice that has stuck with me in some of my most important life decisions.

And as he got up to leave, we asked him for a picture. Hesitantly, he got one clicked with us.

Sunil ji explained later that people misused images with him to make millions.

The fact is, he has remained in touch since. Perhaps because we've never made millions, nor did we learn how to use those images.

14 April 2016
Mohan Bhagwat's first public visit to I.I.M.U.N., where he addressed students at large.

In his various addresses to the organization, I've noticed how he has taken a more moderate stance – from promoting Hindu ideology alone, to saying how he respects all faiths and diversities.

Usually, audience assessment and adaptation is an essential pre-requisite for being a good speaker and no one does it better than politicians. But Mohan Bhagwat didn't pander.

Despite being in South Mumbai, he didn't do what a SoBo would!

The speech was delivered in Hindi, and sticking to his roots.

Did it resonate? Well, you must ask those who were on the other side.

An otherwise decently articulate speaker, I was too nervous about my speech, juggling between Sanskrit shlokas, Hindi and then eventually resorting to English.

But I've found myself pandering in speeches. How to draw the fine line between the two will require a closer examination of Mohan Bhagwats' lectures.

Sunil ji, along with some other RSS pracharaks became very close to the organisation. There are monthly visits to check on us. However, whenever it came to resolving an impasse involving government or meeting BJP leaders, they seemed reluctant.

I have seen people associated to the organisation on numerous occasion – from Subhash Ghai sharing a dais with Mohan Bhagwat in 2016 to perhaps being introduced to the PM and venerated. But I.I.M.U.N. has never been informally or formally introduced.

We are always put under the microscope – are we really going to toe the ideology?

Should we be given more access than what we have?

Why are we into man-making?

So here it is! Yes, we've also produced elected members of the government, and they're in all parties. Yes, we aren't right or left wing; we are an apolitical organisation rooted in centrist Indian school of thought.

And perhaps that's why they are vary of us.

From what I discovered, the real secret of the RSS is to standardize processes via training camps. They organize camps across the country at three levels. The first is the Sangh Shiksha Varg for being introduced to their way of working. The final level camp, which is the Tritya Varsh, is in Nagpur at the RSS HQ. Only after finishing the first two camps can one be invited for the third camp. Typically, all participants are between 15-30 years of age and all instructors between 25-40. I was invited as part of a panel of guests who would preside over this function. It was a matter of great honour.

Previous guests included Former President of India Pranab Mukherjee, Anand Mahindra, Ratan Tata, among notable others. But to all my liberal friends, I was becoming more and more a Sanghi. And to the Sangh. I was perhaps one of the most anglicized India-centric young person they had met.

As I was directed to the accommodation where all the more revered guests had been put up, I was very grateful and thought there may be several modern day amenities. But I realised that it was just two charpoys, an AC and a basic washroom.

Standardization that would put the biggest hotel chains to shame.

Along with more eminent guests like Co-founder of Infosys, Kris Gopalkrishnan, we were taken to see a day in the life of RSS volunteers during this thirty-day camp.

They have to get up latest by 5 am – Now some read this in self-help books and get inspired. We tried to imbibe it with everyone who worked at I.I.M.U.N., but it's easier said than done, especially when you are dealing with a bunch of young independent leaders.

The ones that have followed this rule are more prominent public figures, who have been able to achieve what they aspired to do. And then we have people like me :-)

5.30 am -7 am – attend yoga sessions, march past, learn how to use lathis and other physical activities
On ground activities on an empty stomach?

That too, the first thing in the morning!

Well, for all the fitness enthusiasts, it's a bit like hitting the gym – just cardio, strength and stretches all together!

7 am - 8 am – Freshen up and breakfast. One has to wash the utensils they eat in.

You are then divided into groups; each group is given a task, like cooking.

DIY had a new meaning entirely – cook, eat and clean up yourself.

For all the more privileged South Mumbai and South Delhi kids, I tried to do this at an I.I.M.U.N. Leadership Camp.

Turned out, I was the only one cooking and cleaning up.

8 am - 12 noon – Topics are discussed and explained in Hindi.
It was amazing that people from all states came to attend the camp. But the medium of instruction remained Hindi. And somehow, everyone understood what was being discussed.

It fascinated me, therefore I sat through some of these sessions. I understood that hand actions accompanied the words, therefore becoming the most effective version of the game 'Dumb charades'.

Here was proof that language needn't be a barrier and translators weren't necessary. As long as you spoke your heart, the message seemed to be received.

12 noon - 1.30 pm – Lunch. All meals are vegetarian Indian food.
Yes, for all those who will argue that India is 70 percent non vegetarian, the RSS was only subscribing a healthier diet, something which most doctors would as well!

I am, as you would've guessed, a vegetarian. :-p

1.30 pm - 4 pm – Rest/ Read/ Mingle with people
If I was 16, I would've definitely slept. But surprisingly, I saw everyone in clusters, talking animatedly.

4.00 pm - 6.30 pm – Same routine as morning physical activities

So, if you haven't had enough of activities, here was another opportunity to get cracking!

6.30 pm - 8.30 pm – People debate on different social issues
Samwaad was at the centre of RSS' training.

8.30 pm - 9.30 pm – Dinner

9.30 pm- 10.30 pm – Free time

These camps are week-long, month-long or longer. But even normal days at shakhas/ centres are also similar.

All volunteers work for free, they're taught to lead austere lifestyles with public transport being the most preferred option. Most pracharaks eat at people's homes, but they will never ask for food on their own and some can even go on long fasts if they don't get food.

Reminds me of Jain monks! They're seeking the answer to the spiritual question – *Who am I?* And in this case, the RSS is geared towards nation building and propagating their ideology. But the discipline is the same.

Before proceeding to the closing ceremony, we were taken for lunch with Mohan Bhagwat. Hundreds of volunteers were seated in orderly lines as food was served. We sat on a table right in the centre of all of this with the RSS Chief.

It felt like we were VIPs; people definitely treated him as the first amongst equals.

Now my problem has been this – Why first amongst equals, why the preferential treatment?

As the common man, we've always been at the receiving end of VIP treatments.

But I guess this is common in any company, organisation or political party.

We have tried to reduce it as much as possible with I.I.M.U.N.

Affectionately force-fed, we were taken to the closing ceremony where tens of thousands of young people from different states all performed to commands. Quite the flex. A sight that could bedazzle or scare one into submission. But for those who were present, they were impressed with the seamless synchronization, or so it seemed.

My key takeaway from the visit to the camp was that there was non-pareil diligence, rigour and commitment.

To invoke such values in a cadre that large is a gargantuan task.

The camps were the secret ingredient of the RSS. More so, the reason for their success as per my observation is that those who were in charge led even more ascetic lifestyles. Leadership in any field, whether it is leading your school team in a competition or your co-workers on a project, should be done in a manner which invokes respect in others. After all, respect can't be demanded; it must be commanded. And the best way to do it is through walking the talk.

That is why perhaps Mohan Bhagwat and Narendra Modi are leaders that command lakhs.

Though many questions remained unanswered – funding is anonymously given and that too only once a year, but somehow the organisation sustains tens of thousands of pracharaks.

Yes, they have a separate women's wing, but what about the fact that women do not play a central role in their core leadership structure?

What about their stance on issues such as mental health and LGBTQ rights?

But even for the staunchest of critics, there's a *lot to learn.*

One can't take away from the fact that they treat you like family, visit your homes, participate in your joys and sorrows and, in the true Indian sense, win you over.

The way they embrace you is the same embrace in which the Prime Minister holds world leaders.

And I must confess, *this* RSS has been greatly influenced in the way the organisation has been built by the actual RSS.

I am unabashedly unashamed that stark similarities exist between I.I.M.U.N. and the RSS way of life and that is for all to see.

In a nutshell, the RSS are like oranges. Just like oranges, the volunteers are hard from outside, but can be sweet or sour from within. Depends upon what they make of you! It takes oranges fifteen months to grow and so also for this behemoth to move.

In a world fixated with overnight successes, this organisation and its ideology is a classic example of why everything good takes time. And for something so deep-rooted, the new 'centre' of the country is and will be Nagpur. So better get used to 'Nagpur ke santre'!

Every coin has two sides. In the next chapter, we flip the coin and study the other side. Want to know what I learnt to do/ not do from those who propagated the Gandhian ideology that has dominated the country since Independence? Flip over to see what the Nehru-Gandhi family is like.

Chapter Two

Pappu Ki Pariksha
With *Rahul Gandhi*

Be honest! What's the first mental impression you get when someone says Rahul Gandhi?

It's either that he is an anglicized pampered south Delhi man, who works in a profession that he doesn't want to.

Or

Someone who doesn't understand the value of the legacy of the Congress party and what it stood for. Someone who is simply a mama's boy.

Or

A man who enjoys all things nefarious, such as drugs.

And for most politically sensitized millennials, the butt of all jokes.

As a general practice amongst my friends, if you wanted to call out someone on the ludicrous, bizarre or inexplicable things they did, you would say 'you played a Rahul Gandhi'.

Therefore, going into this chapter, let me confess – I thought he's someone who perhaps didn't have much political acumen. Who definitely didn't have what it takes to unite and lead a country as diverse as India. And nobody can be blamed for harbouring such thoughts, because most first-hand accounts from many luminaries who knew him and society at large were on the lines - *'Pappu ko milne ja rahe ho! Kyu, entertainment chahiye?'*

Many thought I was meeting him because I wanted entertainment. And in such a scenario, I didn't really know what else to think.

Plus, apart from the rampant generalization that society makes of public figures, the nodus with politicians is the fear they invoke in the society at large.

Some of the comments that came my way were:

'He is enemy number one for the ruling party.'

'If Rahul Gandhi is seen associating with your organisation, people will have a very different notion about you all.'

'Top BJP leaders and ministers won't attend your conferences and events.'

And I thought to myself, when the top boss of the RSS leadership had attended, the so-called liberal people had ostracized us and called us stooges of the BJP leadership.

So whichever way you look at it, you were politically aligned in someone's mind. You couldn't control that anyway.

But what really mattered is what we believed in our minds – that we are a non-political bipartisan youth-run organisation.

I must say media can make or break an individual's character and image. The plus side is that I.I.M.U.N. has never sought publicity. As a result, we didn't have to bother about creating an image for the public and media as much. I have closely observed the many perils of being a public figure/ publicised institution. Which is perhaps why I am a firm believer in the fact that you must continue to work and remain invisibly omnipresent.

There are other chapters that will show how this practice hurt us, though in some cases it has definitely been a boon. As you would have gathered by now, the main aim of the organisation is to create leaders without creating noise.

A large part of building global leaders is imbibing in them a sense of belonging to a country which is their identity and their passport to the world. And to that end, I have always believed young people should be exposed to every idea of India, as long as that idea speaks about the nation's interests.

Now when you put all those thoughts in this context, you will understand why this rendezvous was inevitable! To disregard a man in-charge of the political entity that was in many ways the torchbearer of the Independence struggle, would be tomfoolery. Or as my friends would call – it would be playing a Rahul Gandhi.

Therefore, much against the counsel of many well-wishers and advisors, I reached out to Rahul Gandhi's office. Many failed attempts later, I sincerely thought if I was yet again the victim of not publicizing I.I.M.U.N. enough? Or was it the fact that many of UPA's former Cabinet ministers had mentioned to me: "It's impossible to get in touch with RG!"

Could it be true that he did indeed live in those ivory towers and would only fleetingly pay attention to his party and the country? We would soon find out.

Then again, I was no stranger to the world of *pehchaan* we live in.

Despite everything, I wasn't going to give up. In fact, perhaps my only quality which RG later recognized was perseverance.

It was almost four months of not getting a response from a man who most deemed had nothing to do.

On lamenting to a friend in Delhi about the situation, I was asked to write to his close aide, Alankar Sawai.

And true to my nature of being determinedly persistent, I wrote to him.

I have realized, at times it's just about getting the message to the right person at the right time that can set the ball rolling. If you manage to do that, the doors open up!

Whether it's asking your girl's best friend what she likes, or asking the chauffeur the character of the business owner you are about to strike a deal with – the little things make all the difference.

His close aide reverted spontaneously, "Let's meet on your next visit to Delhi."

I was surprised as such alacrity is unusual in a city rife with 'Babu' culture. Standing 6 feet tall, bespectacled, with a greying beard, balding white hair, brown skinned and reasonably fit, I met this IIM graduate in the lobby of a luxury hotel in Delhi. I was quite surprised that he came without any security and that's where I took an immediate liking to his very non-VIP culture.

Frank in his assessment of the Congress party, his boss' plusses and minuses, and so also the state of the country, he seemed like a man on a mission. I explained to him what it is that we were doing. And just like that, a couple of weeks from then, I was having a one-on-one with 'RG'.

The physical meeting was changed to a digital one, and the timing was shifted a couple of times. Which made me think, it's rightly identified as a sinking ship.

My flight was in a few hours, and then on the third and final attempt, we connected digitally. At the very outset, RG apologized for changing the meeting timings. He was most fascinated with what we did and he asked me many a question about the organisation. Quite frankly, it seemed like an interrogation. But then again, this was the norm – people asking a thousand questions and then expressing astonishment or pretending to express it!

During some part of the discussion, I moved towards how I revered Vivekananda. That animated him, and he asked me questions about him and his books, which I thought he wouldn't have read.

After hearing my view points, he passionately disagreed with many.

We then intermittently explored Indian philosophy, Vedanta and some European history. He was definitely a non-linear thinker and kept jumping topics.

But I must confess, for a Pappu, he had much more knowledge than I had expected. A sixty-minute meet turned into a two-hour exchange and time seemed relative to this man.

Amiable, discerning and definitely well read would be qualities I would describe the man with.

Howbeit, the skeptic in me and with the incessant plastering of his image being such, I believed this was an orchestrated rendezvous. As I was rushing to the airport to catch my flight, his aide called me up.

"How was it?" he asked.

After a moment's pause, I answered, "Good! Didn't seem like he's all that unwise as the ruling party makes him out to be!"

This was my honest observation, and I am very courteous and kind in my assessments usually. After all, why offend anyone, and more so politicians! In this case, it was the scion of the family that's been in power for over fifty years!

I can't be sure whether it was my tone or if he read my mind, he knew that I thought all of this was stage managed. I told you he is a smart guy.

Without a moment's hesitation, he offered, "Why don't we do an interaction with your team? Let them first ask questions on any subject, and then he'll talk about a bunch of things – including umm… you guys focus on International Relations from India's lens and leadership, right? So yeah, that!"

I was quite honestly confused and taken aback. Here he was offering me a second opportunity to assess what he believed was India's most misunderstood person. And that too with a bunch of Gen Z leaders! Either Alankar had forgotten his management skills in college or this was a stroke of a genius. I had wanted to invite him to come and speak at a conference, but an unfiltered session with the organisation's student leaders seemed too good an opportunity to give up.

I accepted the offer and excitedly started preparing. We selected seven student leaders across various hierarchies and from different backgrounds and states of the country. Some of their parents were very impressed that RG was going to spend time with them, but there were also some who thought it was an absolute waste of their children's time.

All that said, the student leaders thought this was their chance to be Arnab Goswami!

The unanimous opinion amongst all of them was - '*Pariksha lene mein maza ayega*' and results *ke baad 'Pariksha pe charcha' karenge.* They were all set to conduct an exam, and then enjoy discussing how the student had fared.

Needless to say, the joy when the student gets to be the teacher is a different one.

***

It was going to be a morning session, so we all gathered a night prior to the session and I briefed them about the man we were going to meet. And on me telling them there's perhaps more than what meets the eye, they said, "You are too diplomatic to hurt anyone. Gen Z has a mind of its own!"

Despite that, they agreed to politely probe, but probe they would!

***

Unlike most places in Delhi, this corridor of power is one that all drivers knew. Dressed in smart casuals as we were requested, the eight of us arrived ten minutes prior to the stipulated time. The security called his aide, who escorted us in. As we were entering his office cum residence, we saw a few people from far off – farmers by the looks of it – in dire straits, standing outside, waiting to meet someone. His aide was quick to escort us inside, but he gestured to the guards to see what was needed.

For all you know, it could've been orchestrated, like the Bollywood paparazzi culture. Somehow they managed to get the perfect airport looks, don't they! But nonetheless, they were either trying hard to impress a bunch of young leaders, or were genuinely caring like that.

One simple metal detector check and we were welcomed into his office.

As we entered and were made to sit in a conference room, I observed the surroundings – no ostentatious paintings or over-hyped nostalgia was hanging around the room. It didn't seem that we were seated in the conference room of someone who came from a long lineage of prime ministers.

It seemed just a remarkably ordinary room. Too ordinary, if you ask me. Twelve chairs, a white board and a washroom.

My doubts about image management were coming true. After all, one thing all politicians are good at is optics. And as is the case with every politician, I saw his immediate team hyping up RG's arrival. I've never understood why, though. They're just human beings in flesh and blood and 99 percent of them are not even liked by ordinary people.

A few minutes later, he arrived dressed in a t-shirt and cargo denims, with sport shoes and a mask on his face. As he walked in, he met me and said, "Yet another Shah in Delhi!"

And I said, "Only if all surnames were identities to the character of the person, we wouldn't need to link everything to Aadhaar!"

I've always resorted to humour to crack open a room. Sometimes, it works! But the constant is – I laugh. In this case, Alankar led the way. Kind man! Also don't get me wrong. I think Aadhaar is a fantastic scheme, just the linking process took so long, it made me realise why we're still developing.

And so it began!

Rahul – as he insisted we refer to him – shook everyone's hands and went around asking all of us to introduce ourselves. He asked about our family backgrounds, which cities, colleges and courses we study, and then spoke about himself.

"My name is Rahul Gandhi. My father was Rajiv Gandhi and mother is Sonia Gandhi. We come from a long line of people who have served the country – some who wanted to enter politics, and others for whom it was compulsory!"

Well played indeed!

It's small gestures like these that impress people. The fact that he knew that we knew who he was, but even then bothered to introduce himself was a good ploy.

But the student leaders from I.I.M.U.N. were tougher nuts to crack. They were like all the 26,000+ students before them who have worked at I.I.M.U.N., all between 15-22 years of age, and all having met and interacted with many a luminary. I could see from their expressions that none of them was moved. In fact, a couple of them smirked. Not a good start to the question paper. But then again, there's a reason why Gen Z are the smartest generation thus far.

Rahul noticed my sports shoes and noted that I liked running.

Well, it didn't require one to be Sherlock Holmes, but yes, he was observant! And as Barack Obama mentioned in his book – perhaps trying too hard?!

After understanding that all the student leaders had some or the other leadership role at the organisation – whether it be organising conferences, preparing study material or otherwise – he offered to impart some leadership lessons from his failures.

Everyone took out their notepads. But instead, he got up and took us to a big open green lawn, which I guess separates his residence from his office.

To be honest, all of us were quite baffled.

Rahul Gandhi wanted to play football/ cricket to explain leadership?!

Perhaps the image painted in media was spot on! The man was crazy.

But his idea was to teach us leadership through Brazilian Jiu-Jitsu and the martial arts form of Aikido, in which we later learnt Rahul was a black belt. Now these were techniques that all of us had heard about, but none had ever practiced. As he cartwheeled and jumped to his position, his fitness was visible and I could slowly see the group warming up to this fact. A fit politician is an oxymoron!

For the first lesson, he asked the healthiest amongst us to lock him down, that is, to pin him to the floor. The first lesson was about how when you are locked in by your opponent, you must not use force but wit to outmaneuver him. It's not possible to unseat him all at once. You have to move 1 percent each on the mat, slowly and gradually trying to get into a better position and then when the opportunity arrives, to grab it. In Brazilian Jiu-Jitsu or BJJ, the idea is not to use one arm or both arms to get the better of your opponent, but using the entire body weight.

In any difficult position in life, it is important to stay focused and fight the dodged fight. After all, every dusk leads to a dawn.

The nodus is that most give up as soon as the light goes out and the numbers dwindle; only the valiant few are left. And when dawn arrives, it is imperative to use all your might all at once to make the most of it and unseat your nemesis.

The second lesson was with the leanest volunteer, and in a group that consisted of five boys and three girls, it was no surprise considering my fragile, or as I'd consider it athletic, frame – I was chosen!

He asked me to sit down on the ground and then pushed me from my shoulders. As I sheepishly fell to the ground, I jovially mentioned, "I'm a Shah, but not your adversary!"

As the group burst out laughing, he mentioned that he would show us how to convert energy. He asked me to sit with my knees on the ground, pulled my legs apart and then asked me to lean forward and hold his hands by the ankles. Then he pushed with all his might, and I was asked to push back. With consummate ease, I was able to fend him off.

Sometimes in life, it's not just the amount of energy, potential and ability we have; it's about getting in the right position and utilizing the energy of the aggressor.

We are so often consumed with getting rid of the problem that we forget that there may be a solution in the problem itself. Moreover, not every problem in life can be solved in that very moment.

To explain to a generation that believes in selfies – the right angle and the right light exposure can make any photo 'lit'!

That's all we need to do in life sometimes – change the angle and adjust the light.

And there we have it – countless likes!

These demonstrations went on for about 90 minutes, towards the end of which I could see that the reaction of the group had changed.

From *'iski class lenge'* it was like, *'kya class thi'*.

We took a five-minute breather. Rahul was chatting with his team, and we were all in consensus – this was a unique way to explain leadership!

In using BJJ, he wanted to tell us that there is no winning or losing; there is only learning.

***

I have come across two kinds of people in my life – those who work out of the fear of failure, and others who work because they enjoy their work and are unafraid of failure. The latter take it as an opportunity to learn and grow. Clearly, with the number of haters and badgering he had taken in the polls, Rahul seemed to fall in the second category.

The first part of the meeting had gone well. But had Pappu passed the exam?

The jury was still out!

The next session was the most dreaded one for me – asking him questions. Every time I asked Alankar whether he'd like to see the questions, he kept mentioning, "Don't worry, you guys can ask anything!"

This was an anomaly! In the past, I have seen the most prolific of speakers refusing to start without the questions being shared with them beforehand, and with good reason. I warned him that this may be dangerous – allowing civically conscious teenagers to question and then cross-question.

When the session started, what impressed me most about Rahul was that he kept encouraging the student leaders to ask tough questions. At the very outset, they were looking at me and asking questions. Perhaps worried about the political ramifications on the organisation! But he kept nudging them and said, "There's no senior here. It's just you and me." That was it. There's only a point till which this generation will be deferential.

And so they asked him questions about dynasties in politics, why the congress was failing, the Indian economy, their handling of Kashmir, mental health and many more pointed questions. Some were so piercing that even I flinched!

But he didn't! It was remarkable how he handled these questions!

Gen Z can be an unforgiving bunch, especially when your answers contradict their beliefs.

They question and candidly cross-question.

And whenever he fell short of meeting their expectations, Rahul mentioned that his views and theirs views may not match. That people can co-exist, which is why India survives!

And that is so right! If all five fingers were index fingers, the hand would lose its purpose. Each finger has a different purpose.

One cannot generalize everyone and everything.

Unfortunately, homogeneity is what most leaders today subscribe to.

Unexpectedly, what he said made sense.

The third session was about breaking bread! In this case, Dosa!

As we waited for food, Rahul spoke to the group about their interests from sports to Netflix shows and from history to education. The man was well versed in topics that would interest the youth. I have seen that food can be used effectively to build bridges and this was no different. Apart from the staunchly austere foodie that I am, I could see the other student leaders enjoying their meal and in the process further opening up to him.

One girl even asked, "If I may ask a personal question, why aren't you married yet?"

As we all heartily laughed, Rahul ate some egg-based meal and a Dosa in keeping with his disciplined diet.

Indeed a master class in converting people, or perhaps he was just like this. The more I compare his image on that day and see him conversing over food with students, marginalized groups or his workers, the more I realize that there is good in the man.

But then again, I've realised that there's a lot beneath the surface, especially with politicians. I mean, look at the tax returns they file! With salaries of INR 1,00,000 a month, they drive Range Rovers! In my opinion, this is the most opaque occupation of them all. So I didn't know what to trust.

Session four began with almost four hours over. We were running out of time and I could see all of his staff, apart from Alankar, getting fidgety. It was time for their boss to attend to more pressing matters than dealing with a bunch of teenagers, and rightfully so. In a small room of twelve people, Rahul changed his position and sat on the opposite end of the helm of the table - aka next to me.

So now, every time he had to use the white board, he had to cross over. In a room where we could barely put in one row of chairs, he had to have Alankar get up from the sole chair on the second row.

He embarked on explaining international relations and India. Using graphs and maps, he pointed out how India is in a precarious position and how we must fend off both China and Pakistan at the same time. By now, the group had become so frank with him that they interrupted him many a time and asked him questions. And the ones he didn't know answers to, he kept asking his aide to Google and find answers to.

The man was not afraid of admitting that he didn't know.

That, for a person who is supposed to come from a lineage and background such as his, was surprisingly refreshing.

I noticed that he kept getting up and sitting down. He is very hyperactive and after four hours, even if it were drugs, the effects would've started to wear off! He got up at least once in every three minutes, non-stop for almost two hours on an end. I could see Alankar cringe every time he asked him to move.

As he walked across the country in his unprecedented Bharat Jodo Yatra, I am not surprised at the kilometres he clocked.

Fitness cannot be overrated.

What you define as fitness is subjective. It's your choice whether you'd like to remain nimble on your feet and keep an athletic body type or build muscles and get toned. But I promised myself never to compromise on the kilometres I walk per day and the food I consume.

What, however, was my biggest takeaway was when one of the student leaders asked him whether Kashmir was a situation that they handled appropriately.

"Weren't there many untoward incidents that have happened there under the Congress rule?"

To that, he first admitted that perhaps there were some things that people at various times could've done differently. That not everything anyone does can be a 100% correct. Now such an admission even with that caveat, that yes, his own family and his own party workers and he included have made mistakes in the past, was a very big thing for me.

To admit that you don't know something is a big thing; but to admit that you are wrong, shows a different kind of magnanimity.

And he said it unflinchingly.

He said he was willing to work on his shortcomings.

I have observed numerous of his interactions with the press, media and people in general in the recent past. He has made a mention that he is willing to work and improve his own and his party's shortcomings.

In life, we forget that we don't need to be superhumans.

That even Superman had a kryptonite and that frailties only make you more humane.

In a world where we venerate heroes and think they can do no wrong, we forget that even gods made some mistakes.

To be human is to err.

Unfortunately, many of us want an instgrammable, picture perfect role model and don't truly accept a man in all his frailties.

As he shook our hands and thanked each one of us, Rahul Gandhi had spent almost six hours with us. This, for his immediate team, was a shock and some former senior congress leaders were gasping in dismay.

"Only if he spent that much time with us!" lamented one of them.

The political ramification of this I do not understand, but to want to connect to and educate youth without dabbling into politics, had won the student leaders over. He had taken out time and met with various students across the country, without elections – something that most politicians sparingly resort to before elections.

At the juncture when we came out, they all said, "He's not a typical politician."

That perhaps is his greatest strength, and methinks, that perhaps is the problem.

I have interacted with his team and him on multiple occasions since then. They've asked me my opinion on multitudinous subjects and I've seen him interact with student leaders more than once. Whether it is in the United Kingdom or in India, to pull off an orchestrated script for one hour is possible, but not for six hours!

As I wrapped up my interaction, I realised that one shouldn't judge a book by its cover. And this has further got reinforced over time. When I heard about him walking more than twenty kilometres every day during the Bharat Jodo Yatra, I wasn't taken aback. It seemed a natural progression of what I saw in person. His warmth when he was hugging strangers, the ability to stand and listen to a large number of people made me realise that this was perhaps a part of his personality. An avid reader of newspapers, I started reading between the lines. And I encourage you all to do the same.

There's definitely more than what meets the eye with respect to Rahul Gandhi.

Because of his non linear nature of thinking and articulating, he is often misunderstood. But the thing is, he is surprisingly astute, literate, informed, fit and keen to interact with the youth.

About the future of the Congress party and electoral politics, I do not know. Whether he is a *tapasavee* or not, again, I do not know.

But literally, in my book –

Pariksha mein Pappu pass ho gaya.

Ab jao pariksha ke result pe charcha karo!

Albeit having passed in my book, one man continues to maintain that Pappu is buddhu. Many say that this man is single-handedly responsible for polarising a nation. Some say he is a CIA agent, others coin him as a megalomaniac, and some see him as a messiah. Let's find out who Subramanian Swamy truly is!

Chapter Three

The Cost of Truth with *Dr Subramanian Swamy*

Growing up, the school education system taught everyone how to follow the norm. Whether it be elocution techniques of putting your hands behind your back, or maybe just giving marks to those who were good at rote learning!

Those who were rewarded should have been reprimanded; and those who should have been rewarded were relegated.

India achieved independence in 1947, but the country has not truly become independent. We've had generations of Indians becoming conformists. Most of us follow the system and some select privileged ones *become* the system. It's the pragmatic and accepted way of life.

But not anymore.

Gen Z is challenging status quo, they are breaking stereotypes, they are not ones to take instructions mindlessly, with their heads pointing downwards. In my observation, whether it is an instruction in school or a religious ritual at home, they don't hesitate to ask '*why*'.

Society brands such people who do not conform to existing

patterns as outliers, as misfits. Some say they are mavericks and others call them geniuses, but everyone in unanimity will tell you – they are people who are a difficult bunch to deal with.

Ask me! We are run by teenagers, and those in their early twenties!

But this is exactly what the Indian society needs. People who ask questions.

We need innovators and trendsetters who can use our rich legacy to pioneer in every walk of life. That way, if you are 'abnormal' according to societal standards, then don't worry! You are the new normal!

If we face difficulty in accepting such individuals today, then just think about the situation some fifty or sixty odd years ago.

Born in Mylapore, Tamil Nadu in 1939, this Tamil Brahmin (Tam-Brahm) has been an eccentric recusant all his life. I have some Tam Brahm friends and all of them are unnervingly smart. I thoroughly enjoy putting all of them together in one room. After all, they all think they're smarter than the rest.

But read this chapter, and then we'll decide if this gentleman deserves to be smug.

***

Born to a statistician father, mathematics was in his genes. Having completed his Bachelor's Degree in Mathematics from Hindu College, Delhi, he pursued a Master's Degree from Indian Statistical Institute, Kolkata. Following that, he went on a full scholarship to study a Ph.D. in Economics under a Nobel Laureate at Harvard University. And while he was at Harvard, he did courses at MIT.

Now when you get those many degrees from as many prestigious schools, it's difficult to remain grounded.

This man then went on teach at Harvard University, before leaving a lucrative job to occupy a chair on Chinese studies at the Delhi School of Economics. His appointment was nullified because he didn't subscribe to the views of the then ruling dispensation.

I hate it when politics gets involved in academia. The two should be kept miles away from each other. With doing just that, we would've solved half the world's problems.

Unfortunately, politicians want to dabble in everything they can!

And this perspicacious scholar then became a tenured professor at IIT Delhi. He also taught for the longest time at the Harvard Summer School, until he got removed from there as well!

All that aside, his most notorious exploit, by which the world introduces him, took place on 10th August 1976. At the height of the Emergency in India, when all opposition leaders were jailed, he fled to the United States of America.

And despite an arrest warrant being issued in his name, he miraculously flew into India. The Vice President of India was chairing the first day of the Rajya Sabha session, when – much to the disbelief of all his fellow parliamentarians – he walked inside.

The obituary list was being read out. As soon as the Chairperson finished reading out the names of those who had lost their lives, our man stood up and said, "Point of order. You've missed out on one name. You should have added democracy in that list."

He then fled via train to Bombay and from there to Gorakhpur and then onwards to Nepal. On a chartered flight from Kathmandu, he left for the United States of America.

That was one of the most daredevil things that any rebel could do! Had he been caught, he would've been jailed. Or perhaps worse. Such is the cost of truth.

But as Gen Z would put it, he winged it!

The next day, the foreign press reported it as first page news.

Emergency in shackles: Young parliamentarian sneaks into and outside of India.

He became the face of India's resistance to oppression. He became the hero in disguise. Dr Subramaniam Swamy.

***

The Chief of the Rashtriya Swayamsevak Sangh (RSS), Mohan Bhagwat, had told me in 2017, "You remind me of another person who speaks his mind. The only difference is, you speak in private; he speaks in public. You must connect with him. You will enjoy his company."

Dr Swamy's image in the minds of many in the Core Council of the organisation was that of an ultra nationalist. His radical stance on Muslims and homosexuality made some feel nauseous. Many thought he didn't regard two hundred million Muslims as part of the country and this was surely unacceptable.

And here was Mohan Bhagwat telling me, "You will enjoy his company."

Now before judging the situation, please understand my background. Despite being a Jain by birth, my eating habits are Islamic.

I eat only in the morning and in the late evening, I celebrate Christian festivals with aplomb, and in today's day and age, I find that Gautam Buddha's middle path can offer much in life. But at the end of the day, I practice Hinduism in day to day affairs. And I refer to the scriptures which gives meaning to the lives of all Hindus – the Vedas.

I don't know as much as scholars would, but a few readings of the Vedas are enough for one to understand that the books say that there is only one Divine Consciousness. And that one must continue to learn from everyone, see the good in everyone. After all, we are all but one. But the view that many held was that Swany did not see people with the same lens.

Now, try explaining all this to Gen Z leaders, for whom such 'bigotry' and 'hate mongering' wasn't pardonable at all.

I will be honest, it took me weeks.

By then, we had invited the right wing ideologue Mohan Bhagwat. And now, we were going one step further with someone who people say is even more heretic in his stance. I lost out on a few friends I had because all of them thought I was converted. And those who didn't, presumed I wanted to contest the 2019 Lok Sabha elections on a BJP ticket.

There's never been a doubt in my mind – no politics for me, but look at the optics! I couldn't blame them.

Fortunately, my team understood me (or had no other choice, who knows!). By the time we wrote to him, which was early 2018, he had by then been a six-time Member of Parliament. Basically, he had been in parliament for longer than I had lived.

He has served as Union Cabinet Minister for multiple portfolios and is regarded as one of India's finest public 'intellectuals' (a term he despises). Or, as some would say, an absolute nut job!

We wrote to his executive aide, Jagdish Shetty.

Picture a bespectacled man, standing at 5 feet 6 inches, with a healthy paunch, thick black handle bar moustache bordering an imperial moustache (for my desi friends – picture the one that Veerappan had).

To complete his typical sarkari look was a bald head with some grey hair on the sides. When we met him for the first time at a coffee shop, he was surprised to know the reach of the organisation, where its former members were and how we impact students.

He was a very sharp man, and observed everything – from the watch I was wearing to the way I pronounced words; from the way we presented the organisation to patiently going through every last page about us. He was thorough in his work.

"Dr Swamy doesn't go to very many new places or organisations, but I am happy to bring him to some of your functions. By the looks of it, you don't seem to have any personal ambition," said Jagdish ji.

I was relieved with his assessment, but to be honest, I too had a personal ambition and that was to learn as much as one could.

This was my real life B-school.

Jagdish ji and I soon became friends and he served as my Wikipedia. Though I don't know of what value I am to him, I realised that just by virtue of being with Dr Swamy, he had picked up on so many things.

A conversation with a knowledgeable person was as good as reading a hundred books. Here, I have tried to give you both – conversations, in a book!

"Can we meet him to invite him to our annual finale conference in August 2019?" I asked Jagdish ji.

I.I.M.U.N. puts together a four-day educational extravaganza where the crème de la crème of school students congregate from all across the globe in a city close to Mumbai. The most decorated speakers are called here and we had decided that Dr Swamy would be the keynote speaker for the event.

And so I went to Delhi to meet Dr Swamy at his residence. He had a simple house. But had a Z security apparatus large enough to occupy a small island nation.

As I entered his home, a fair but diminutive lady, towering in every other way politely said, "You must be here for Swamy."

And as she ushered me in, I met man's best friends. The dogs were also as excited to meet me as I was to see them.

In the living room, I saw a humongous television and books in every place there was space. A few sofas and long tables dotted the entire area which was adjacent to a rectangular dining table with six chairs.

"Can I get you a cup of tea or coffee?" asked Roxanne.

"He's here for conversation, not for tea or coffee. Aren't you, my young friend?" Entered the man, 5 feet 8 inches, with balding black hair, a clean shining forehead, big long ears, kurta and pyjama, no old age flab, fit as a fiddle!

If I didn't know he was 80, I would've passed him off as a 60-year-old for sure.

The dog had found a new a toy in me, and only when Dr Swamy warned him did he stop.

"Jagdish speaks highly of you! So tell me, what is it that you do?"

And that's when I narrated the entire story.

As I mentioned to him that we would love to have him as keynote speaker, he shot off, "Why not Chief Guest?"

"Because sir, ... umm...Gen Rawat is going to be the Chief Guest."

"Okay then, no problem! Anybody, but that Moadi!" (And that's how he pronounced Modi, not me!)

Mind you, here was a sitting Member of Parliament, a member of the BJP, and even still he didn't mind speaking his mind about the fact that he didn't like some of the policies of the Prime Minister.

People in the opposition were worried what would happen to them if they overtly criticised Narendra Modi, but not this man.

I inquired why he was so against the man, especially given the fact the he works harder than any other PM, or such is the notion.

Dr Swamy quipped, "He's good for himself and his friends, the economy is nowhere it's supposed to be! Look at the rampant unemployment in the country! He's deserted the Hindu cause, he only has yes men next to him..."

A ten-minute monologue made it clear that he was miffed at the man for choosing the wrong people for ministerial positions. But even more so for what in his opinion was a mockery of the people's trust in the party.

Now, in my assessment, it could also be that he didn't get his due. Swamy had in the past supported Modi, and at a time when he was rightly supposed to be given a portfolio and his knowledge put to use, he was shunned.

I have observed a common malady both in ordinary folk and in the most decorated luminaries – expectations. We expect things from our near and dear ones, from those who we help. It's always a quid pro quo or at least a thank you from them.

I have had numerous such experiences when I have gone out of my way to help someone and not received as much as an acknowledgment. I will be honest and confess that it infuriated me. Whenever such a thing happens, I positively reaffirm myself by saying, "The best expectation is to have no expectation at all!"

To do good without any desire, is the purest form of existence. However, easier said than done. I still can't practice it.

***

Many months later, a sixteen car convoy entered in a procession which left the security at Aamby Valley City in a tizzy. They carried automated weapons and brazenly entered through the gates. For the General Manager's "Rules are rules! We will need at least twenty-five minutes to make a meal," all accommodations were made for Dr Swamy.

That makes me wonder, have you observed the behaviour of people changing when it comes to VIPs?

Even in cases when you are a plain-clothed person vs you are with someone who is a public figure.

For a country that is obsessed with celebrities, we seem to forget that every ordinary person is a celebrity for someone.

Treat everyone with the same respect, or on a lighter note as Dr Swamy does, with equal disdain for both Moadi and Congress.

As I welcomed him at his villa, he sat me down and asked me, "So tell me, I've got a speech prepared, but I would prefer to do a longer Q & A!"

At that juncture, I was worried! During most conferences, majority of the student participants are well-versed with current affairs and history, but here was a man who had not just *seen* but *scripted* history. And he, at times, was very dismissive per se. We wanted to create a good impression on him and also not scare the other participants off. That's why the idea was – a monologue would be better.

For all its good qualities, Gen Z listens less, is very opinionated and is also quick to go on the offensive. Perhaps, it's more a teenager thing and less a generation thing. My younger sister was a classic example. She would do exactly the opposite of what I asked her to. And then complain to my parents. And I would get reprimanded for no reason. Annoying little sibling! Anyway, before I digress, so I tried.

"Sir, post your speech, how about some questions from the moderator?"

"No, I want to talk to the children."

"Sir, but they're 13-18 years of age," I reasoned.

"Yes, and they're our best hope to challenge the bondages of society," he emphasised.

"How about we select a few from before and have the moderator ask?"

"Don't diplomatically try to manipulate me into saying yes!"

I had no choice. I wasn't going to succeed where almost all lawyers had failed. It was pointless arguing with this man.

Sometimes it's better to accept defeat, lose the battle and focus on the war. Getting fixated in the moment can hurt you. Look at the larger picture. I messaged the Core Council (the senior-most set of individuals in the organization) to carefully preselect questions.

"Okay! Now considering you've brought me here, I will give you a chance to ask me a few questions."

I had always been intrigued by the political Tom and Jerry show. Swamy vs Gandhis. Swamy had been forced into exile by Indira Gandhi, only to then be requested to lead a delegation to talk to the Chinese. According to his own admission, he was friendly with Rajiv Gandhi and often met him late in the night.

"Just one, sir. Why are you always after Sonia Gandhi?"

"She is a thief! A power-hungry woman, she is a KGB spy, a murderer! She isn't an Indian by any stretch."

I knew about most allegations. I knew he called her thief because of the National Herald case where since 2011, Swamy had filed a petition that the Gandhis had benefitted to the tune of INR 5000 crore.

Power-hungry because she apparently went back on her promise and pulled out support from a government that Swamy had stitched in the 1990s.

The KGB spy who engaged in illicit activities was another conspiracy theory he had weaved in the early 2000s, but murderer? This one I had no clue about.

"Murderer?"

He then went on to tell me how she had apparently played a role in murdering people in her own party who would have gotten in her way. Now, I've heard of politicians putting Chanakya's *Arthashastra* to good use – *saam, daam, dand, bhed.* By any and all means necessary. But this seemed too far-fetched.

Then again, as I have come to realize, nothing in politics is far-fetched! People will do anything for power. Murder on every side of the political aisle is common. A thing I can't in the wildest of my dreams ever resort to.

This remains one of my biggest inhibitions for young clean people to join politics. Then again, no revolution is easy.

Nearly fifty percent of the members of the 19th Lok Sabha have criminal records. And worst, some even have cases of terrorism on them. Now imagine if we could wipe them out! Not the cases, but these kind of people, from the parliament?! I encourage you to join, or to at least cast your votes diligently. That's the best way to cleanse anything, whether it be your gut or the system, from within.

***

Swamy came on stage to a thunderous applause! He said India can only be great because of its youth, its children, as the politicians are all peddling their own agendas.

Well, I couldn't disagree to that statement. One thing I admire about him is that he is an honest politician in both, his answers and so also his conduct.

Post the interaction, a young boy asked, "Are you upset that you didn't get your due?"

"I'm upset that India didn't get its due. And yes, put the finance minister in front of me and I will let you decide who should be in charge of the country's finances!"

Another girl asked, "Why do you think Prime Minister Modi isn't appointing you as the Finance Minister?"

"He is scared. If I become the Finance Minister and do well, people will want me as PM!"

And then he asked the girl, "If you were the Head Girl, would you appoint a smart senior who is opinionated as a part of your school's decision-making committee?"

"If she was going to contribute to the schools success, why not?" she answered.

Swamy clapped. So did the audience. This man knew how to get the desired reactions.

Naive. Pure. Energy. = Youth!

The Q & A round went on for a longer time than stipulated, but the students seemed to be enjoying it. Here was a man who was speaking the truth – no filter, no camouflaging.

The teachers and principals flinched, but the students loved the numerous 'mic drop moments'.

No wonder the man has over eleven million followers on Twitter.

Truth is enamoring! And especially when presented with flair and panache! Remember, try sticking to it; it'll hold you in good stead.

As I led him outside, he asked me, "Good job, Rishabh! What's the plan for the future?"

"Sir, glorified school teacher, producing more leaders who unite the world, the Indian way."

"The Hindu way," he added

"Ummm…"

"We must chat," he said, exiting the venue.

And then he proceeded for a meal with my parents. My dad is an admirer of his and so also of the Prime Minister. Otherwise reticent, he jumped at the opportunity of meeting a man who he said should work with Modi to form India's dream team. Ask some of my team and they would give you looks that could kill.

Swamy eats only simple chapatti, sabzi and dal. Austere in his diet and his mannerisms, he sat down and spoke to my parents at length. He is fond of Jains and took a liking to my parents.

My parents told me later, that despite all his intellectual superiority, he is – as Gen Z would call him – very basic.

I have seen him dine many a time and therefore can vouch for this as well. He eats very simple food. And eating habits speak volumes about a person. Some like Swamy eat to fuel their bodies, and on a lighter note, others like Jagdish ji and I enjoy indulging in delicacies. I'm not saying it's wrong to enjoy the meal, but I've noticed that most successful people eat the same constant food with very little variation.

A bit like one of my favorite characters, Sheldon Cooper from one of the legendary sitcom *Big Bang Theory*. Okay, go on! Judge me, like you haven't already! But just imagine, he wasted no time on food or clothes and had a set routine on both. Eventually awarded a Nobel! But then again, he too was a maverick.

I guess it all boils down to what you want to do with life. Okay, too philosophical. Getting back.

Dr Swamy invited me for the launch of his book *Reset,* in which he talks about radical reforms like abolishing income tax. A populist measure that would definitely make the salaried and middle class happy, its economic viability is hotly debated. During this time, the border skirmishes with China were increasing. However, what was surprising is that the Consulate General of China was present for the event. Swamy's mandarin connection has been long standing, and his knowledge about them is unrivaled.

He explained to me later, "It's rightly said, keep your friends close and enemies closer. Keep a check on them! What are they doing, why are they doing what they are doing, and what will be the future repercussions of their actions?"

Let's be honest! How many of us do this? Follow the arch nemesis from the spam accounts?

After the book launch, he did a signing and patiently sat through the entire queue of a few hundred people wanting an autographed copy. Of course, he loves the adulation, but more so, understands the need to connect with people.

As an introvert navigating life in an extroverts' world, I've often grappled with this gremlin. Being socially amiable is a life skill that one must develop.

Swamy since then has on various occasions been kind enough to grace the I.I.M.U.N. HQ of the organisation and has passionately spoken about a host of issues. My most memorable visit was when he got riled up and started arguing with a former Core Council member about Hindutva.

As someone who fought for the Ram Mandir, numerous temples and now Ram Setu, here was a fervent Hindu nationalist vs a Gen Z leader.

The latter vociferously argued, "Why build a temple or a mosque? Let's build a school. Allah and Ram will both be happy!"

Swamy is an educated man himself, but mentioned that "Certain things are about beliefs" and dismissed the issue with "I don't know which side of the fence do you stand on?"

He later asked me, "I would like to speak to that boy."

The boy wasn't ready to speak to him, though.

Swamy was showing an open mind. But the student leader wasn't.

Dialogue is important. Most problems in the world and in our life take place because of breakdown of communication. Don't they?

Remember, keep talking! I mean, not like me, but you get the point, don't you?

For a man who gets up at 5 am, Swamy has a habit of taking a sixty-minute siesta. On one such occasion, as he was resting at my residence, he came out in twenty minutes.

"Help me prepare," he said.

He was going to various programs, and needed a research assistant. Considering I had time with him at home and this was a personal setting, I asked him a question that I wanted to know the answer to, since the first day.

"Aren't you worried, sir?"

"Worried about what, Rishabh?"

"Going after people who are so powerful."

"Why should I worry, they should! I don't have any skeletons in my closet," he said laughing out aloud

"Sir, what if they come after you? There's nobody behind you. I mean, I know the RSS are friends, but still..."

"See Rishabh, RSS or my friends or even my wife will not fight my battles. They are *my* battles for a reason. I believe that if I have the desire, I have the ability."

That is so true.

He's not a lawyer by qualification. But you see, from Sushant Singh Rajput's case to suits against previous governments, he's successfully fought and won every case he's filed. In 2019, he even won a case against IIT Delhi for incorrectly castigating and throwing him out in the 1970s. They had to reinstate him and pay him fees along with 18 percent interest in full settlement. It takes time, but Swamy eventually wins.

In this statement, he taught me a very valuable life lesson – you don't need anyone to help you out. Yes, a kind word, a helping hand is good. But all of our battles – mental and otherwise – are ours to fight alone. And if we believe in ourselves, the battle may be something we may lose, but we'll always win the war. An 82-year-old economics graduate with no formal knowledge in law is showing the way.

We were travelling together from Delhi to Gangtok on what was my first charter flight for I.I.M.U.N. Swamy reached before us. We entered the aircraft and as I sat opposite him, I knew the man had to suffer me for a while. We were trapped on an aircraft with nowhere to go.

To be imperturbably candid is a quality I have rarely found in people, but more so in luminaries. They have to be careful about what they speak about others. They're always worried about image management. I don't blame them – I have seen up close what happens when they voice their opinions. Inevitably, their professional life gets boycotted. But here was an anomaly – someone whose professional career thrived the more he spoke the truth. Or did it?

"Dr. Swamy, your life trajectory would've been very different had you not blamed Modi for everything," I said.

"I don't blame him for everything. I think he's done many things correctly as well. It's just that I can't be a silent sycophant."

"Respectfully, don't you think that if you were silent on some issues sir, he would've taken you in?"

"No point in sacrificing the truth! It is a bitter pill to swallow. Like I keep telling you, you can't change the system from outside, Rishabh."

"Sir, but you could make so much of a difference! Is it worth it?"

"It's the cost of truth, and I am ready to pay it!"

A heavy cost indeed.

Yes, we aren't all cut out to be mavericks.

But how many of us have rote-learned without understanding the meaning?

Or slid a note to the cops just to get out, even when we didn't jump the signal?

How many of us have blindly followed the norm?

We all can't be Swamys, but we can definitely challenge the system in our own imperceptible manner.

Swamy has led his life with unmatched moral righteousness and will go down as an honest politician who was in every way an outlier.

I won't lie! I too could not keep the same standards right through my tenure as President of I.I.M.U.N., but as soon as I stepped down, I promised myself that I want to be a Swamy. Thus, this book, an honest assessment of some of India's most powerful people. Nothing but the truth!

From one man who loves the RSS to another who was castigated for accepting their invite! But true to the bipartisan image of the office he held, some feel it was a good decision whilst others think that he betrayed his ideology. Either way, it's not often that a make-believe President gets to meet a real President. And for my part, that was enough.

Let me take you to Lutyen's Delhi.

Chapter Four

A Presidential Address with *Late Former President Pranab Mukherjee*

Growing up, especially as children, we are always beguiled by stories. I fondly recall my grandmother narrating me bed time tales. The stories always started with... "A long time ago, in a faraway land, there was this king..."

Like most children, I was also fascinated by the plot and enamoured by the king and his coterie. How he administered it. How he grew the kingdom. What he did with it.

Akbar and Birbal were my favourites.

The thing with childhood stories is that they keep coming back in one form or another. Like little girls who hear about their prince charming and boys who hear about the princess! As we grow up, some of us are always looking for them. I can confidently say that my fascination with kingdoms continued well post my childhood.

History was a mystery for me, but every time the history lesson spoke about Ashoka, Napoleon, Alexander and even monarchs like

Elizabeth, my eyes would light up. I would patiently listen, on the edge of the chair.

Methinks, I was a king in my previous birth. :-P

Now in the modern context, this kingdom would be a country and the person who led it would be the Head of Nation.

I am sure you are well aware that different countries have different types of government. USA has only one all powerful position, aka the President; United Kingdom has the Prime Minister and then the sovereign, ie the King; India being a Republic has both the Prime Minister – who is in charge of the Union Cabinet and running the government, and so also the President – who is the Head of Nation and also the Commander-in-Chief of the Armed Forces.

The locus standing in India is that the position of President is considered ceremonious. But I've always been a firm believer that one cannot function without the office of the President.

Take for example the extra judicial powers given to the President to grant amnesty to those who have been awarded death penalty.

Or that all bills can only be passed after the assent of the President.

Even the Prime Minister is appointed by the President.

One can, of course, argue that the President would do things only on the recommendation of the Prime Minister and the cabinet, but, there have been occasions when the President has acted on their own behalf.

The fact that the first citizen of the country is the Head of the State, always made it a position I wanted to know more about. Besides, they lived in the palatial Rashtrapati Bhavan. Who would miss a chance to go there?

But it's not that easy. You shoot off a letter to the President, inevitably you don't get a response. I mean I don't blame the Secretariat! They must be getting thousands of letters from all across. But, I have personally felt it is pivotal for those in positions of power to be able to have a cohort of intelligible people in charge of communications. It is imperative! And I say this because the ideas and perspectives from the grassroots can change how those from their high windows will measure the world.

I had at the very outset of I.I.M.U.N. written to the rocket man of India, Former President, APJ Abdul Kalam. I was told and had seen him visit the smallest of schools and colleges. It was said that he was very fond of young people and children. But unfortunately, I kept writing to him and didn't receive any response.

Perhaps, we were only in our initial years and with little credibility, how and why would you trust nobodies? Or maybe the messages weren't going to the right person.

We implemented the plan of having a team who would sift through communications at I.I.M.U.N. For every nine spam emails, we used to get the one that would become a talking point in the weekly apex decision body meetings. So, if you are a public figure or an organization, try this and see the change! If you are an ordinary person like me, then I'm sure that you'll have all the time to respond to correspondences.

In India, there are many politicians, but few statesmen. Very few who have defined India as much as this man has. He has been a seven-time Member of Parliament, the only Finance Minister who has presented budgets before and after the Liberalization reforms of 1991 and has famously said to have almost become the Prime Minister twice. Nominated at a young age of 35 into the Rajya Sabha, he was a close confidant of Indira Gandhi. From her entry into politics in 1997, he was also responsible for mentoring Sonia Gandhi. Awarded the highest civilian award in the country by the Narendra Modi government, he was a man who had the gift of taking everyone along. A quality which is a pre-requisite for any successful leader.

In 2016, buoyed by our initial success in inviting several chief ministers and governors, I first wrote to the 13th President of India, H.E. Pranab Mukherjee.

I've learnt that it's not just about writing to the office, it's also getting in touch with the person who shares the same wavelength. Whilst he was President, he had a secretarial staff of very many erudite people, some of whom had been with him for over decades. But, when personal assistants have personal assistants, then it becomes a cumbersome process.

By the time we wrote to Pranab Mukherjee's team, I thought we were in a position to at least elicit a response. But the universe had other plans. The problem is – you can't just enter Rashtrapati Bhavan to hand over an invite.

In 2017, after many failed attempts, we finally got in touch with his OSD, or as they are called Officer on Special Duty.

This girl sounded very professional, had a youthful voice and seemed to be keyed in to the conversation. "A young girl such as yourself doing so incredibly well speaks volumes about you! So happy to have found you," I was genuinely happy.

Now you call a girl younger than she is, you'll feel you're in the safe zone.

Not flattered by my remarks, she said, "Please resend the email on this id, and also speak to Mr Rai."

Mr Rai was his right hand man, the person who controlled access to the President. A well-known fact in Delhi.

Many days later, I was connected to Mr Rai.

"Right now, he's caught up, Rishabh. Perhaps in a few months from now?"

When we started out, I used to get infuriated whenever someone used to tell me this. It was hard enough to connect to people, but then they'd say things like, not available for a few months,?!

Over a period of time, I realized that all these people were very busy. And in their priority list, we came at the very end of the pecking order.

By 2017, I wasn't any stranger to waiting for months on an end.

To put it in cricketing parlance, it was just like a Test match and not a T-20 game. One had to play out the good overs and wait for your opportunity.

But in this case, the wait didn't seem to end. In July 2017, just as Pranab da was finishing his term as President, I sent a few reminders as a last ditch effort to remind his team that we exist. But to no avail.

As he moved to his new residence, ailing health was cited as one of the reasons for him not contesting for the next term as President.

I don't usually give up, but in this case, I left it as is. For no other reason but the fact that I didn't want to trouble an elderly gentleman. I knew how much effort it took my grandparents to undertake tasks that weren't in their priority list. I dropped a polite email to Damini, stating – "Please let me know when he gets better, we would love to host him at I.I.M.U.N."

And a few weeks later, she called me and said, "He's started seeing people now. Why don't you come and see us?"

Now I didn't know whether this see 'us' was meet Mr Rai and her, or see Pranab da. Either way, I wasn't giving up on what could be an opportunity of a lifetime.

Yes, we have over the years corresponded with, received support from and even hosted various Heads of Nations, but to be able to meet one in person! Now that would be exciting!

But as a Core Council member and I boarded our flight to Delhi, we didn't get over excited for a journey which could simply be an introductory meeting with his team. I had learnt not to keep any expectations. We reached Delhi, only to realise that the aircraft delay, along with the snarling traffic jams, had left us behind schedule.

We informed Damini that we were running a little late, and she said, "Rishabhhh! What's wrong with you?! You are meeting Former President!"

"I'm really sorry, just reaching. We have come all the way from Mumbai. Please, please don't cancel the meeting!" I pleaded.

Since then, I've always booked a flight at least one day in advance, especially when attending scheduled meetings. On a lighter note, the word please has a charming effect on Delhiwalas. I don't think they hear it too often in their city. :-p

And so it worked! She changed our meeting slot.

As we reached his residence cum bungalow, the security rushed us in. Perks of being late. But no! Don't try it.

What if our meeting had been cancelled?! The tone of this chapter would be very different!

We were made to wait in a small oblong waiting area, with a kind officer of the Secretariat by the name Mr Chopra offering us tea/ coffee. He sat at the head of the room at a desk which was adjacent to the door we entered from. A room faced Mr Chopra's right hand side.

Whose cabin was that, I wondered.

And then I shifted my gaze to the rest of the place. Some chairs and a sofa on one side along with a computer screen on the other, and a couple of clerks working on something. I tried to see what they were doing. I had a habit of studying the surroundings; they tell you a lot about the person. Or that's what reading Sherlock Holmes taught me.

"They're booking Former President's tickets," said Mr Chopra

Embarrassed, I pulled up a chair.

On the opposite end of Mr Chopra's desk and a couple of stairs above the waiting area was where Damini was seated. I had never been to a President's office. This was all very new and exciting.

Dressed in an Indo-western double plated jacket and unkempt hair, I looked at Damini.

She muttered, "Rishabh?!"

"Yes!"

At five feet six inches, round, curly hair and a happy face, she must have been in her early thirties at best.

"You are a kid!" she said.

"No, I'm not. I'm 26!" I retorted.

"Haha! Okay okay, you are 26, and I'm the Queen of England!"

Now, it helps when you look genetically young in places, but in important places and even recreational ones, it's a bane. Like when I was 22 years old and went to Las Vegas, I had to show my ID card for almost everything! But now as I get older in age, looking young has its perks!

"So we are going to first meet Former President and then we'll meet Mr Rai," she updated us.

And in that moment, all other feelings dissipated. It was here! My first in-person conversation with a Head of a Nation!

"Thank you!" I said, beamingly.

***

Former President's room was one that had more books and less space. He sat behind a desk on a raised chair, with a huge television facing him. Two chairs faced the head chair. The pictures of Pranab Mukherjee and the man in person are identical – bespectacled, gray hair and 5 feet 4 inches tall.

He was seated as he said, "Please come," gesturing towards the chairs. Damini left us.

"Can I get you some tea/ coffee?" he offered, and I could hear the heavy Bengali accent.

"No sir, just meeting you is an honour in itself," I said.

"So tell me."

"Sir, can I speak frankly?"

"Yes, please tell me."

"Sir, I will speak frankly… President to President," with a dramatic pause.

I tried my humour. It didn't work. Or so the Former President made us feel. After a moment of awkward silence, "Ahh President, I see!" he chuckled.

Phew. So I've spent a lot of time around someone who I believe is the funniest man in India, Cyrus Broacha. And I would like to believe that I have picked up a thing or two from him. At times I realise I haven't. :-p

As we explained to him what the organisation did and handed over an invite for the August event, he interjected, "Yes, you shouldn't have called it Model United Nations in the first place. The UN limits the scope. It's better that it is India's International Movement to Unite Nations!"

We then spoke about how changing the name leads to a mindset shift.

"But not how we do it in politics," he laughed.

A career politician, he too it seemed despised some practices of the political class. I didn't disagree.

Concluding the meeting, he said "I will attend and gladly herald a name change."

I wanted to jump in joy and hug this benevolent man. Thankfully, my team member held my hand and concluded the conversation. We clicked a few pictures and tried to calmly walk outside.

"You can be excited, you know! I am a President, after all!"

I immediately fell in love with the man!

"Haha thank you soooo sooo much sir. This means the world to me!"

He read the room, the situation. I am sure he could immediately tell the excitement in my eyes, the animated fervour in my voice, and notice the spring in my step. Even at the very outset of the conversation, he may not have liked my sense of humour, but he understood it. The thing with those who are very experienced is, they are all very good judges of body language.

Most of us just see a person; experienced people see *through* you.

Imagine, if you could study the body language of your interviewer and tailor your response basis what he felt towards your answers! Or understand whether the girl you are crushing on is reciprocating or not.

If you are in school, college or are a young adult, I cannot emphasize enough the need to master this 21st century life skill! Study *kinesics,* or as we popularly know, the art of body language.

As I walked outside, I excitedly told Damini, "It's done!"

"No, it's not! It's only fifty percent done."

She took us to the mysterious door next to where Mr Chopra was seated.

Mr Rai was a serious man, dead serious.

Towards the end of our conversation, when I jovially said, "So Mr Rai, what is your *rai*?" smartly playing on the Hindi word to know his opinion, not one smile.

I have met straight-faced people in life, who don't have a funny bone. That's an issue, because you need to use some other emotion to break the ice.

I later realised that it's not that he wasn't a funny man; it's just that he was very serious about his work. Such people are very committed and dedicated to what they do. Hardest nuts to crack!

"Is it done?" asked Damini

"No! He said this is promising, but we'll have to see how it pans out."

"Don't worry! Let me see what can be done," she assured.

We left, our hearts full of hope and faces brimming with happiness.

We had just met the Former President of India!

A couple of weeks later, I received a call.

"Rishabh, he really wanted to come, but can't," said Damini.

I was despondent. And in that moment, all the grand plans I had made, sank.

"I am just joking," she chuckled.

"What?!" I almost shrieked.

"Yes! Former President has agreed to attend, and is very excited about addressing you guys," she happily concluded.

I jumped with joy. Literally.

As we began preparations for what was going to be an iconic evening, even the property that we were hosting him at repainted and spruced their hotel up! It was a momentous occasion for everyone involved! Schools, principals, luminaries, former team members, all were informed. Not surprisingly, we had more people and less space.

And then, just two weeks before the event, Damini called.

"I am sorry, I have bad news. Former President isn't keeping well. We can't risk Pranab da's health. He's cutting down on programs for the month," she told me in a rather grave voice.

"Good one, Damini!" I wasn't going to fall for it again!

"It's true Rishabh!"

"I have a lot of preparations, got to go," I said and hung up.

And then she called again. She had sent official communique. This was the biggest moment of I.I.M.U.N. – our full form changing. I couldn't process it.

I gathered myself and asked, "I am sorry to hear about his health, but is it that serious?"

"No, but we aren't risking it. No travel, no commitments; only bed rest."

What can you say when someone states that their medical condition doesn't permit it? I understood the predicament, but Damini could sense the dismay in my voice.

"I'm sorry Rishabh," she offered kindly.

We had become friends by then, chatting about the sun, moon and everything politics. She knew my happy and sad voice by now. And she knew how sad I was.

As I gave this news to the Core Council, they reacted in an identical manner. We had to contain this news, both from his security standpoint, but also from the event perspective.

Then one of them asked, "Can you tell sir to give us a recorded message?"

I was a little more ambitious. I called Damini.

"What if we set up a video conferencing facility and have people watch it live?" I asked.

"No! He hasn't done anything like this before. He's not done video conferencing before."

"We will set it up, don't worry! Shall send a senior to Delhi. Don't worry, we will be able to make it happen," I persuasively mentioned.

"No, Rishabh! It's not feasible. Plus, his health... perhaps a recorded message at some point, in case he is well?"

Now most of us don't ask for the ridiculously obscene, do we? We are always satisfied with the ordinary. The thing I've realized is that if we shoot for the stars, only then at some point do we fall on the ground. That's something I have attempted to do all my life. But, in this case, I really wanted the northern star.

"Let's prepare for a live address. If his health permits and doctors allow him, let him do it! Else, we can always do a recorded one, which we can play in the closing ceremony?"

"Rishabh... umm..."

After a moment's pause, she said, "Let me speak to Mr Rai."

About two weeks later, we were setting up Former President's first live video conferencing address post his tenure at Rashtrapati Bhavan.

These were pre-COVID times, and do remember that we are a bunch of teenagers and at best twenty-something-year olds. The 'engineering' students volunteered and we did a few tech checks, took a secured line and put a basic set up in place. Spectacularly brilliant in my opinion! And all we could now do was pray!

Remember where there is a will, the way will open up!

Many of these student leaders were using this equipment for the first time in their life, but had miraculously managed.

A day prior to the opening, Pranab da was in better health. He had started moving around again and the universe was conspiring to help us. As the day arrived, Damini called.

"We are doing this for the first time, Rishabh. Make sure everything goes seamlessly, else I am going to lose my job, and you, your life!"

It was happening!

I went up and introduced the man. And for the thousands of student participants, 200+ I.I.M.U.N. team members and the dignitaries and Board members in attendance, we will always remember his words:

"I now declare Indian International Model United Nations to be India's International Movement to Unite Nations!"

Truly a presidential address! And so the journey began.

Some moments are priceless; this was one of them!

The thing is that despite all the hard work, the final one percent wasn't in our hands. Call it fate, luck, divine help or whatever you believe in, but I have realised that you can only do 99% of the work. It is best to remember that the remaining 1% isn't in your hands. If it happens, thank the universe, and if it doesn't, it will happen when the timing is right! But the important thing is to keep at it!

After the event, Pranab da was very happy being associated with the organisation. Requests of meeting him, or for that matter, talking to him were always something that were entertained.

One such fond memory was when I had visited him with an Advisor of the organisation. Ambassador Prakash Shah – perhaps the most revered and decorated Indian diplomat alive – had expressed the desire to meet someone who he had the good fortune of working with. And coincidentally, the conduit was there!

That day I remember him telling me, "Pranab would remember me and would have readily agreed to meet had I called! But you have done a wonderful job!"

Well, as you know, I have a personal agenda – whenever all these people talk, I take mental notes. Some of those, I have shared in this book for you.

"Prookash, kemcho?" said Former President.

"So happy to see you Pranab bhai!"

As two old friends chatted away, I realized that there is a lot that they had in common. Both had varied opinions about the government, the current politics, the economy and everything else. But they allowed each other room for argument. They shared many laughs over anecdotes which I had only read about in history books.

"You know Pranab, my father was in business. He told me, if someone insults you in the civil services, just come back! But I liked it so much here! I was flying with Indira (Gandhi), advised three PMs, visited the Kremlin and the White House. I have had quite a life, only you've made the wrong foreign secretaries all the time."

"Like how they selected the wrong prime ministers," the Former President retorted.

They both laughed. But in that I observed the unfulfilled desire. Or perhaps it was that they were over it and therefore could joke about it.

Former President was touted to become Prime Minister twice, most certainly in 2004, after the Congress-led UPA had come into power. And the same was the case with Amb Shah. But the men were casually laughing about it. I observed that in the moment of things, even the greatest of mortals have the same issues. And in that thought, I realised, I don't want to be this.

After so much of what Gen Z calls 'hustling' and achieving what others could only dream of, and doing a remarkable job at that, there was still room for more. It's like at the end of a hearty meal, there's always room for dessert, and we keep stuffing ourselves.

But the truth as I've learnt in life is that one doesn't have to stuff oneself to the brim; it's better to be content with the basic.

You'd say that is one of the biggest dichotomies of life. True, because that's something I am still grappling with.

In my many exchanges with Former President, another thing that surprised me was his yearning to learn. From Vivekananda – who we both were great admirers of – to everything about Indian polity, our rendezvous would be filled with him asking me many a question and opinion. And that for a Head of Nation was pretty unusual!

This remarkable quality of having childlike curiosity is what kept him so informed. I once asked him, "Sir, you have so many people to ask. Why do you ask me questions?"

"I ask everyone, Rishabh," he replied. "Your perspective is different from Damini's and from Rai's. I want to get a sense of understanding of the same issue from different peoples' standpoint."

That was a thought that stayed with me. How many times do we seek to go beyond and learn – from our peers, colleagues or juniors? We are usually content in our own assessments. Perspectives, unsolicited or otherwise, aren't something that we are big on. In this regard, he was different from most other politicians I had met. They usually were most interested in giving their opinions. I promised myself to seek perspectives from everyone and to be open to ideas.

Damini called me one day and said, "Former President is planning to go to the RSS function in Nagpur. He'll be sharing the stage with Mohan Bhagwat. What do you think?"

Now, when people as important as these meet, it's bound to be front page news. But in a country where fissiparous tendencies were only increasing, this was much needed. I knew both men had very different ideas of India, but both dearly wanted to see their motherland achieve great heights.

"He must go. After all, it's another perspective! And if there is one thing I have learnt from Pranab da, it is that one should take into consideration all perspectives. Isn't that what makes India what it is!" I repeated his lines.

Many from his own party criticized a move that should have been seen beyond the myopic lens of politics. I, for one, was thrilled. We needed more of this.

A year later, he was rightly decorated by the government.

As of February 2023, he is one of the forty-eight Indians who have been conferred the highest civilian honour, a Bharat Ratna.

31st August 2020

The country came to a standstill. Not just because a veteran politician had died, not just because a Bharat Ratna had passed away, but more so because India had lost one of its finest statesmen.

It's the stuff presidents are made of.

Humility. Integrity. Loyalty.

A man who valued different perspectives – Former President Pranab Mukherjee.

May he rest in peace.

From someone who served as President to someone who was nominated by another President for exemplary contribution to Indian sport, she has become an exemplar of public service in her short stint in Delhi. To stay on track in this field is often more difficult than staying true on ground. But is there space for good people in a city that has more bureaucracy and less democracy? Turn over to find out!

Chapter Five

Boarding The Payyoli Express With *PT Usha*

Every time there's a sports event hosted, whether it be in school or at any other level, we usually see two sets of people. One category of boys and girls would prepare and look forward to showcasing their athletic prowess. Then there are others who don't want to get out of their houses and enjoy the day as an off! I have always been in the first category. Cricket, volleyball, chess, running or swimming – as long as I win, it doesn't matter.

Even when it comes to my attire, I am always dressed in track pants and t-shirts and that was way before athleisure became a thing! It is the norm. A tradition I have been proud to continue.

Basically anything that involved or emanated from or because of sport was exciting.

All that said, there was an overwhelming number of people who just watched cricket in the name of sport. In a cricket frenetic nation, the conversations always centered around Sachin Tendulkar, Rahul Dravid or Sourav Ganguly.

I grew up at a time where other sports were not even given pages worth of coverage in newspapers, leave alone making biopics on players' lives. If you asked urban young people back then, who the captain of the national hockey team was, they'd draw a blank. I leave it to you to imagine that if this was the state of the national sport, what must be the state of others.

Our exposure to sports started to finish.

However, one did read about some names in history books. For instance, there was the great Milkha Singh in track sports, Dhyan Chand in hockey and Leander Paes in Tennis.

Unfortunately, that's all most of us knew.

As an event organiser, I always faced a gargantuan challenge with people from the sports fraternity. They always charged a ludicrous amount of money to attend.

Many sport managers told me, "Movie stars will need promotion, politicians will need audiences, but people from sports don't need any of this. The famous ones know their face value, and the not so well-known ones live off government grants, and therefore need the money."

To be honest, every field echoes such problems. For most luminaries, it's either money or some powerful person asking for a favour. Only a few do things altruistically, and even fewer for young people or nation-building. Even in case of the latter, most prefer to do it via a government program, and not a nameless private initiative.

I don't blame them. If you extrapolate this, it is the same with our lives too. We are always attracted to glamour and perhaps we will do something for those who come with a reference. There are very few who'd go out of their way to do something for strangers. But the most altruistic and open-minded people I have met have always told me that when the opportunity arises, we must too. It can make someone's life.

In our case, to make matters worse, we have always been a youth-led organization that has worked on constricted budgets and without reference. If you want a clearer picture, think of college fests without sponsors.

Quite naturally, with this as the delimiting factor, our approach was met with great resistance. Yes, the odd sports superstar did attend, but it was far and few in between.

I remember discussing the issue in the Core Council meeting. A staunch feminist mentioned, "Rishabh, we must add more women leaders to the Advisory Board."

"I couldn't agree more."

"Then why didn't we, in the past?"

A valid question. And it's not that we didn't try. But in a male-dominated society, most powerful positions are yet given to men. In most cases, we write to everyone. It's just that in some cases, not even one writes back! One of the many perils of functioning as a low profile organization, I think.

Now the main purpose of the Advisory Board – as the name stands – was to advise! And to share perspectives on various issues that the organisation faces. The year was 2018, and by then, it was a venerable cohort of erudite people. To add anyone to the list, the person had to not only be someone who had many a story to narrate, but an ideal role model for Gen Z. So we wrote to a few people.

And in that list, there was this one name which I was most impressed by. A small town girl who had risen from a remarkably modest background to become a beacon of hope for young people across the country.

The year was 1984. Just a year before this, Kapil Dev had led the Indian Cricket Team to win the World Cup by beating the revered West Indian giants. The country was yet reveling in the moment. However, something happened at the Olympics 1984 in Los Angeles, which changed Indian sport forever.

The sprint queen of India was competing against the best of the world in track sports. For someone who could not afford a pair of shoes to now representing India, her journey had been remarkable!

She started the games by clocking 56.81 seconds in the 400 metres hurdles heats. Thereafter, she went on to clock 55.54 seconds in the semi finals.

In the final, she came fourth, clocking 55.42 seconds – just 1/100th of a second behind the eventual bronze medallist.

The country was salubriously euphoric!

In the true sense, she had broken the glass ceiling in many ways.

Later, she went on to win many medals at the Asian Games, Commonwealth Games and National Championships, amongst other competitions.

She became the reason why many entered track sports, and why girls started thinking about sports as a career.

It was one of the first few times that a nation recognised a sport apart from cricket. And the reason was – PT Usha.

I wrote to her. Instead of her management, fortunately, I received a reply from her husband, Srinivasan.

Try reaching out to the person themselves, and you will be surprised how many of them are completely contrasting to their managements! Though in this case, both the management and the person in question are incredibly sweet.

At 5 feet 8 inches, an almost developed black handlebar mustache, slightly dark brown complexion, Srinivasan reminded me of a Tamil movie star. And who, like many of them, enjoyed his food and politics.

His discipline in responding to me probably stemmed from the austere life he lived, whilst in the Central Industrial Security Force (CISF).

He said in a heavy Malayali accent, "Yes, Rishabh ji. We have received your email. Let me speak to Usha and get back to you."

A few weeks later, I sent a polite reminder.

He had a few questions, which I addressed on a phonecall. Another few weeks passed, and we were still waiting for an answer.

Now in most cases, people don't pursue the matter if there's no update. I have come to realize that most times, till you don't get a definitive no, there is still a glimmer of hope. Whether it is your dream school or the job interview you didn't hear back from – try novel approaches. Till you get a definitive no, don't give up!

You know, the final stretch is usually the hardest. And beyond that is victory.

That's exactly what I did! I sent another email reminder to PT Usha. A fortunate stroke of serendipity later, I received the email.

I do not know what happened. I am not usually like this. It has been a lot of unexpected work. I am sorry. It is an honour to join your Board.

Regards,

PT Usha

As always, reading the name in the unread emails had me adrenalized. But what struck me was the fact that she had apologised for the delay. This gave me an insight into the kind of person she was. She could have simply confirmed with a general 'yes, I am glad to be a part of the Board'. But this showed the humility.

It's not difficult to apologise. This is that one word that can solve personal issues, professional conflicts and even wars! But the ego doesn't allow it. And I am no one to preach, I myself am learning the value of actually meaning and saying 'sorry'.

Now, I did have the opportunity of talking to PT Usha on call on multiple occasions, but had never met her in person. It was August 2021 when COVID decided to give humanity a break. As we put together our first hybrid Annual Championship conference at the iconic Taj Mahal Palace, Mumbai, it was a concourse laced with many firsts.

As a practice at the organisation and more so out of compulsion and less out of choice, all luminaries are always flown in business/ first class, put up at five star hotels and travel in luxury sedans.

Srinivasan ji called me up and said, "It is a short flight. We'll prefer to come in economy."

I was momentarily disconcerted. No guest in the history of the organisation who had come for the first time had said these words. Most – after seeing what I.I.M.U.N., does and how we do it – have changed their approach entirely. But celebrities or their managers have often berated young people on the fact that the room category should be a higher one, that the person shadowing the guest should be more trained, the food should have had extra salt and what not!

"No Srinivasan ji! I insist that we have you travel at least from Bangalore in business class. Vistara and Air India both have great connections."

"Not necessary! We will do a car from our place to Kozhikode, and from there an IndiGo flight connecting to Mumbai via Bangalore. Why change airlines and all?"

Now most of us are victims of chasing the better life and sometimes splurge when it's not even necessary. But this is the difference between those who have come up the hard way and those who have had it easy.

Every rupee counts.

My parents still travel everywhere in economy for the same reason. I didn't realise it when they kept telling me, but I did when PT Usha behaved thus.

Again reiterating the same lesson – often, those closest to us are trying to impart the same lessons, but we shut them out. Howbeit, when someone else, who we admire, validates it for us, we implement it. So to all teachers and parents trying to get their children to understand things, use this method and see how quickly we learn.

***

PT Usha reached the hotel late in the evening.

As she was settling in, the team apprised me, “She’s in the room, RS!”

Yes, RS! By 2021, my name had changed from Rishabh to President to RS. On whether it was an abbreviation for Rishabh Shah or Rishabh sir, please ask Gen Z. They are kinder to me than they are to the English language! I mean, the word ‘good’ became ‘gd’, which eventually is just ‘g’. As long as they don’t respond with ‘.’, I can still understand some part of what they say.

As I entered the room, I saw that the hotel staff had put some pictures up in the room and a few other details personalizing the place. Trust Taj to go the extra mile! As soon as I entered the room, she stood up in attention.

Dusky skinned, she was 5 feet 7 inches tall, but seemed even taller for some reason. Of course, her achievements, but perhaps it was the pair of shoes she was wearing. Wearing tracks pants, a t-shirt and a sports jacket – give her a whistle and she could make all of us start running there and then!

“Meet this young man! He is the Founder & President of I.I.M.U.N.,” said Srinivasan.

“Very nice to meet you sir,” said PT Usha.

I was startled.

“Ma’am, I need to call you ma’am and sir, not the other way around. It is an honour to meet you,” I responded

And it was true! She was the one who had accomplished things. I, on the other hand, was just about starting out.

I am sure you have noticed by now that PT Usha was incredibly modest.

If someone wouldn't point out that she was PT Usha, she could easily have been mistaken as just another person. No airs, no trumpets! But what left me smitten was the respect that she exhibited towards everyone, right from getting up every time she saw me to thanking each team member she interacted with.

I had to actually go and tell her to stop. "Ma'am, you don't need to get up every time I come into the room." I was quite honestly a little embarrassed by this sheer display of respect.

"You have achieved so much at such a young age; this is the least I can do! Plus, you are our host."

That last part was it!

"Ma'am, then I will just have to stop entering rooms that you are already present in," I said.

We both laughed, and she stopped getting up thereafter.

Now on most counts, whether it is business, government, cinema – luminaries don't get up to greet people, and I don't expect them to! But the respect that it accords the host makes them feel special. After all, they are the ones hosting you.

Whenever someone makes the mistake of inviting me as a speaker, I always stand up when the host walks in. The thing is, that's the least we can do. I have often used this practice as a humility barometer to check who stands where.

Now PT Usha's public conversations were all in the form of moderated talks. Someone who spoke only as much was needed. She reminded me of Barack Obama, someone who measured everything before saying. However, unlike Obama, I don't think she enjoyed conversing as much.

Some people think and talk. I talk and then think! Maybe that's why I am writing about them. and not the other way around!

She had two public interactions – one with me, and another one with inarguably India's most prolific speaker, Dr Shashi Tharoor.

Srinivasan called the I.I.M.U.N. member assisting him and said, "We must ensure that she has answers to all questions prepared properly. Your audience should get the desired outcome."

They had asked for the questions beforehand, but they wanted to doubly ensure that she had perfected what to say and how to say it. She wasn't worried about maintaining political neutrality or anything going out on social media; she was genuinely interested in ensuring that the students would learn something. Such kind of attention to detail is prodigious. I mentally made a note of getting her to meet Chairman of HDFC Deepak Parekh – the two of them would really get along with each other. Connect people; together we can achieve so much!

I've seen people being passionate about things, but for someone who was docile in everything else to suddenly speak with great gusto was completely unexpected.

As we ventured towards the topic of making athletics a compulsory part of schools, you could see the spark in her eyes!

And this passion and energy to create new PT Ushas is something she is pursuing silently, with her own set up for the not-so-privileged girls.

She told me post her session, “What pains me is that today we have all the facilities, we have coaches for different kinds of training – mental, physical and what not – yet we are not able to get enough gold medals for the country!”

“Why do you think this is happening, ma’am?”

“Because this generation is extremely pampered,” she said. “We weren’t even given basic shoes. My coach used to tell me to run barefoot, illness used to be taken in our stride, we used to be a tougher lot.”

Despite being from ‘this generation’, I could not help but agree to what she was stating. It was on point – cent percent. We are definitely better off in terms of access to resources than the previous generations.

But somehow, think about it – how many new industrialists are created in this millennium? And I am not talking about unicorn founders who have sold their companies to foreign investors.

Despite the BCCI becoming the richest sports body, we haven’t won a World Cup in over a decade.

For that matter, how many songs in cinema have substance! We are more likely to find a different kind of substance in the songs.

Call me old school or an old soul, but there are many things I admire about millennials and Gen Z. But then again, some things were much better in the years gone by.

Generously accepting that there are always some exceptions to the norm, what separates this generation from the previous is perhaps that they were ready to sprint in the marathons and we want to sprint in 100 metre races.

Standing true to my faith in the middle path, I feel imbibing the best practices from across generations would perhaps be the best policy.

***

The Advisory Board meeting took place on 15th August 2021. As everyone came together, the conversation was on expected lines. The more active vocal advisors spoke most of the time and others contributed briefly. When you have so many important people in one room, it becomes imperative to ensure that everyone gets equal time. Now, I had gone to PT Usha twice in the meeting, and both times, she simply said, "Yes, it is good."

I was perturbed. Post the meeting, I spoke to Srinivasan ji and asked him, "Have we done something wrong?"

"No no, don't worry! Usha only speaks when she knows it is adding value. Why waste words when she cannot make a difference? This is her first meeting… as she learns more about the organisation, she will speak her mind."

Now here was a lady who was confident in her own skin. She was sitting at a table with some of India's most important people, but didn't feel the need to validate her credentials. I have seen new advisors wanting to pass a few witty remarks or wanting to do something to catch the attention of the remaining members of the group. But in this case, nothing.

This small observation made me understand that we spend half our lives preparing ourselves to impress people. Then the other half goes in impressing people. But why do that, when you have come alone and have to go alone?

And that's why, in this regard, Gen Z and those younger would relate to PT Usha more than I did. They don't feel the need to impress.

A few months later, we had an I.I.M.U.N. concourse in Tirupur. The team was deliberating on who to invite as the Chief Guest. The first name on everyone's list was PT Usha. She had won people over with her conduct, including the ones that didn't know her. I rang up Srinivasan ji.

"Everyone is a fan now, sir. Can she come for our Tirupur conference?"

"As long as she doesn't miss more than one day of the training," he confirmed.

"Oh! Training for?" I asked, wondering whether this was a second innings.

"She is training the girls, right? But tell me, when is the conference?"

For someone who had achieved so much and was retired, Usha could deservingly take a couple of days off. But she is passionate about ensuring that another girl wins and gets back the medal she couldn't. And to that end, she would do everything in her hands to enable and empower them. Her life dream, as she had reiterated many a time, was to make all non-cricketing sports reach every part of the country. She wanted to win maximum medals for India in the Olympics. This intensity and commitment after reaching such heights is hard to find.

Everyone works for themselves, but the greatest kind of service is to work for others. PT Usha was and continues to be at the forefront of such service.

I am fortunate to have met teachers such as these and I touch their feet whenever I meet them. Whether it be my math teacher, Parashar, who gave up family, friends, social life and centered his life around students; or my English teacher, Mrs Doris, who travelled during the Mumbai floods on 26/07/2005 from another part of the city. This, on a day that most south Mumbai kids couldn't travel three buildings away.

There are simple ways to be grateful for such blessings. Remember to acknowledge such teachers who give their life for you. And when life gives you the opportunity to teach someone, impart selflessly.

As for our Tirupur conference, the only way for PT Usha to travel was either to undertake a seven-hour car journey, starting early in the morning to enable her to reach on time, or to charter a helicopter.

Most people would have politely excused themselves. I don't know of a single luminary to have travelled this far, in a car. And in that I realised what sets her apart. Time is money, but she said, "I will be able to finish whatever work is there whilst in the car."

Where there is a will, there will be a way. And where there is no will, there will be excuses.

As one of the Core Council members told me, "Her conversation and conduct were exemplary, as always. However, the incident she narrated made me realise why we should feel honoured and lucky to live in the same era as PT Usha."

"Can we go shopping before I leave, please?" she asked the team member.

"Of course ma'am, I'll be happy to take you. Where would you like to go?"

"Any factory outlet of a shoe store please," she mentioned.

The assumption was that she perhaps needed a new pair of shoes. As she entered the shoe store, she decided to pick up 40 pairs of shoes. Puzzled, the team member asked, "Who are these for, ma'am?"

"For my children at PT Usha School for athletics!"

Again, she could've easily bought things for herself, but chose to put others before herself. The shoes could help transform the lives of the girls and propel them to achieve great things for the nation.

"In my early days as an athlete, I didn't get all these facilities. Therefore, this is the least I can do," added PT Usha.

Think about this: How many of us give back? Especially to those who aren't as privileged as us? As per a HURUN report of 2021[2], for a country whose culture speaks so much about giving back, those who are in the net worth of 50,000 crore and upwards donated only about 0.09 percent of their wealth. While the corresponding figure in China was 1.48 percent, and 2.52 percent in USA. Now, it doesn't matter whether it is one rupee or ten thousand rupees; the important thing

2 https://theprint.in/india/indias-rich-got-richer-in-covid-but-share-of-philanthropy-fell-says-report-on-charity-trends/881751/

is to donate to a cause we believe in. Start today, it could make a huge difference to the not-so-privileged.

***

As the news broke of her being nominated into the Upper House of the Indian parliament, I called an excited Srinivasan ji.

"This is amazing! Thank you for all your support," he said jovially.

"It's all her achievements; we have done nothing," I added after passing on my best wishes.

And I meant it. I don't know whether it was her meeting Mohan Bhagwat in 2021 at I.I.M.U.N. or the fact that she was always being considered. But then again, why had it not happened before?

I was glad that someone who has done so much for Indian sport was finally getting some recognition!

Not much good may come to the organization due to our apolitical nature, but at least people associated to it were in a better position to do things for the country that they loved so much!

In my humble opinion, the biggest announcement for Indian sport was made on 10th December 2022. The state of non cricketing sports is improving, but we aren't a fraction of what we can be. Since sending our first delegations for the Summer Olympics in 1920, for a country with 1.6 billion people, we have won only 35 medals in over 100+ years. This shows the amount we invest in sports infrastructure.

PT Usha had once shared her thoughts on the reason behind it. She said, "People are not getting enough facilities at the grassroot level." That is true. I am most certain, people in administrations in the past also wanted to do good for sports, but somehow, corruption in the system gets the better of the plan.

Under Narendra Modi's governance, some bold decisions have been made. Problems can be solved by someone who has experienced them first-hand. When you empower honest, well-intentioned people and put them in charge of things, they will contribute to nation building!

Think sport. And who better?

PT Usha was elected unopposed as the President of the Indian Olympic Association.

As Srinivasan ji picked up the phone, I said, "She always wanted to change the face of Indian Olympics sports."

"Yes, and the big man asked her to do it!" exclaimed a proud husband.

I was happy, but also worried that she may become another sportsperson in the middle of this bureaucratic mess that Delhi is.

"Sir mentioned that he will support Usha and provide her with whatever is required," added an elated Srinivasan.

Finally, after several years and various governments – including eight years of the Modi government – she was where she deserved to be. Where the nation needed her to be.

Most people change after they become famous, gain access to wealth or power. But not PT Usha! After all this also, she had the courtesy to call in and say, "Sir, sorry for not coming for your Board meeting on 10th December 2022. The elections were on the same day."

"Of course, I understand, ma'am. Srinivasan ji told me. And please, just please don't please call me sir."

And we all cracked up.

During my most recent visit to the Indian Olympic Association, Srinivasan ji took me to the President's office. As we chatted about everything unrelated to sport, he told me about PT Usha's dream for the place.

"Athletes used to come and stand in a queue at the back door of the building. Whether you had won nationals or won a medal, you were made to wait your turn. The bureaucracy was in charge. She wants to transform that and allow people to come in through the front door."

"Athletes should be allowed through the front door and the bureaucracy should be made to wait their turn," I added sarcastically.

And just as I said that, an elderly gentlemen in his mid-eighties came in, lamenting about some pressure he was receiving. Well, whether you are eight or eighty, the red-tapism and corruption is a menace which is difficult to escape. I felt bad for the old man.

She entered the office, and we all got up. I was seated at the head sofa, a place which she would most certainly occupy and therefore moved aside. But she went to this man and consoled him, reassuring him that the issue shall be taken care of.

Then she greeted me and said, "More than two hundred files are pending, but the meeting today was good."

The press then entered, asking for her reactions on various issues. She circumvented the twisted political questions and spoke about her life's passion – of ensuring that India wins maximum medals at the Olympics.

From a person who barely spoke, she had blossomed into a prolific speaker. No wonder she's anointed Deputy Speaker of the Rajya Sabha.

As we sat to chat about multifarious issues, she was interrupted by someone or the other who wanted to see her, every five minutes. Unflinchingly, she let everyone come in – whether it was her staff who needed some extra space to work from, or a state association president, or an athlete. In the 90 minutes that she spent with me, she must have seen at least 15 people. Whilst 99 percent offices in Delhi believe in a closed door policy, here was a lady who was defying the convention!

A family friend of theirs who was in the room spoke about how they were offered a bungalow in Delhi. PT Usha had rejected it, because she preferred to stay in a flat.

"It's small and easier to manage," she was quick to add.

You don't need to be a politician; for most humans, more is also less.

And here was someone for whom less was more. Quite sufficient.

I must not forget to mention here the role that Srinivasan ji plays. I have seen him with her at every station that the Payyoli Express took a halt at. He was the person who responded to our first communication. Even at the Indian Olympic Association, he was waiting for her in her cabin. In a world where definitions of feminism change as per convenience, he is a rock by her side. A great example for everyone who is looking for a good role model to show their sons!

It is often said that behind every successful man is a woman. I must say, that behind PT Usha is a selfless Srinivasan ji!

People say this is Prime Minister Modi's era, some say it is China's era, I say we are lucky to live in the era of PT Usha. May the Payyoli Express bring us many medals from Paris, Los Angeles and beyond!

Part II
Other Fields

While those in public service may be some of the most powerful people in the country, there are those who were/are at the helm of their respective fields and yield the same, if not more influence. These people control some of the most important things in our lives – like what we consume in the form of content or in some cases how money moves across the country.

Some were responsible for keeping our borders safe and others use music to unite the world, the Indian way. However, one commonality that binds them all is, they are some of India's finest ambassadors and are patriots who have dedicated their life to building the nation in their own way.

And what better than to start with someone who gave his life for the country. Turn over to find the story of India's first Chief of Defence Staff, Late General Bipin Rawat.

Chapter Six

A Man Of Honour
Late Gen Bipin Rawat

As you would've gathered by now, one of the main aims of the organization is to sensitize tomorrow's leaders to the idea of India.

People define India in ways that are best suited to them. Politicians define it in conforming to the ideology that they are promoting at that time of their career; others on the basis of their experiences and how they perceive the country.

However, if there is one set of individuals that eat, sleep and breathe India, it is the Indian Army, Navy and Air Force.

Undoubtedly, the Indian Armed Forces are the ones that can truly speak about what it means to be an Indian. They are the real heroes of our country. They literally give their today, for our tomorrow.

As someone who is so passionate about India, I cannot imagine how it took me up until 2016 to realize the significance of the Armed Forces. But then again, that's how much of a colonial hangover we have as a population.

In any film coming out of United States of America or United Kingdom – take for example every Mission Impossible or James Bond movie – the Armed Forces and the country's defense/ intelligence apparatus are venerated. Haven't you seen at least one such Hollywood film in your life?

Now tell me how many Indian war hero films have you seen prior to 2016?

Four, maybe five?

And cinema isn't to blame alone.

In other western democracies, civil society also decorates them; they are treated with respect. It is a matter of great honour to have someone from your family serving or having served in the Armed Forces.

But in what is the world's largest democracy, and despite the wars they fought up until the Kargil War, the Armed Forces were always treated second to civilian leadership, and sometimes second to local law and order enforcements. The problem here is that they're not accepted as the real heroes by the nation.

As many Chiefs who have served under different administrations explained to me, "There is a much more deep rooted problem. The people don't feel as patriotic."

I agree, A.R. Rahman's *Maa tujhe salam*, or Shah Rukh Khan acting in *Main Hoon Na* may evoke some passionate fervour. And if neither arouses you, India winning a cricket match against Pakistan most definitely will! But we were always apologetic about being Indians. I remember going overseas in the late '90s and stereotypes against Asians being glaringly visible.

We were the land of snake charmers.

One thing I must give due credit to this government for is that the rampant jingoism has given rise to a generation of Indians who are ready to take the world head on. I.I.M.U.N. started spreading the idea of India in 2011, and this government only came in 2014. However, their narrative in this specific regard furthered our cause.

And since then, the country has evolved. Virat Kohli wears his passion for the country on his sleeve and is unafraid in sledging back when sledged. Neeraj Chopra and PV Sindhu have defied all odds and are household names. On a lighter note, Ranveer Singh even wears Indian curtains on his body and sets global trends.

India is fast-changing and Indian-ness is fast-spreading. And that has let generation Z feel that yes, they can! A sense of pride of where we have come from and where we are going! What's obviously helped is the demographic dividend. A median age of 29 means a lot of the workforce is coming from India.

As this buoyant spirit was further spreading, I.I.M.U.N. was doing its bit at a school level, in its own infinitesimal manner.

I remember how schools flinched at the thought of a Lok Sabha or a Mahabharata being simulated in a Model United Nations conference, but somehow being completely okay with a Model House of Congress or Mock American Civil War Cabinet.

Unknowingly, cloaked in an Indian disguise, we furthered a powerless institution even more and took it to 220 cities. But thankfully, in 2017, shed the tag of a failing United Nations and became India's International Movement to Unite Nations.

How I wish we had done this in 2011 itself. Every school today wouldn't have Model United Nations; they'd have our version of a Movement to Unite Nations in their school. The intent was right, and now we're fixing the problem at a school level.

At an I.I.M.U.N. Core Council meeting in 2016, we were discussing how people from various walks of life were attending I.I.M.U.N. and speaking about India. Then one of the student leaders raised a valid point, "Rishabh, why not invite those who serve the country at our borders?"

"But will they be prolific speakers?" asked another.

"Doesn't matter! They'll have real-life stories of serving the nation, better than these cheap politicos," said the girl.

A unanimous vote later, it was Game. Set. Match.

Since then, every I.I.M.U.N. city team has endeavoured to get someone from the Armed Forces to their conferences. Schools resisted it at first, some still do, preferring more glamorous names per se.

But things are changing and we owe special thanks to Indian cinema for producing more number of movies on the Indian Armed Forces in the last 7 years than in the last 70. This thought has now permeated all sections of our society.

Now, the thing about most luminaries is that it's easy to track them down. Whether it be via the internet or otherwise. However, in the case of Armed Forces personnel, neither Google nor teenagers who pride themselves to be human googles (stalkers, basically!) could find any way to reach out to the Chiefs of the Armed Forces.

And then one intern told me, "Why ask people only in Mumbai? If Mumbai can't solve it, doesn't mean people across the country couldn't!" Simple, but brilliant.

Only if the governments would learn to do the same, they'd realize soon that the real talent of the country is definitely outside of our metros!

We sent out an email to the first official id we received – that of the Indian Army Chief, Gen Bipin Rawat. Now the thing with most government offices is that no one responds, more so to a bunch of young people, who do not use references.

To my utter disbelief, I received a call within 24 hours of my email from the Army Headquarters. It was an acknowledgement.

"We have received your email. It has been forwarded to the concerned officers, and they will get in touch with you soon."

In no time, just like that, I was talking to someone in the Army! He did the normal interrogation, but it is at that time that I realised how vigilant the Indian Army was. They asked for all the details with reference to the organisation – pecuniary and otherwise. Along with documentation, records and pictures of all guests that had attended, they needed much more than a generic organisation profile.

But considering they were asking for more details meant that they were seriously contemplating it. I remember sitting till 2 a.m. with some Core Council members, sifting through our records and compiling the necessary documents.

And then, there was radio silence for a few weeks.

You know the feeling that you get once you've studied hard, given an exam and now are eagerly awaiting the results? That's how we felt. But in our case, we didn't know when the results would come out. Every day, we hoped it to be that day.

The day finally came.

"Rishabh ji, I am calling in from the Indian Army HQ. Is this a good time to talk?"

This is why they're men of honour. No government officer asks a civilian if it was a good time. They automatically assume.

"Yes, of course!" I responded excitedly.

"You have been granted a meeting with Gen Bipin Rawat whenever you are next in Delhi," said the operator.

What? Are you kidding me?! I was ready to take the next flight out! And so a date was fixed. It was early 2017 when I met him for the first time.

Delhi has been one of my least favourite cities, and this has more to do with the pollution and the VIP culture and less with the common man.

I had never been to an Armed Forces office, leave alone the very HQ of the Indian Army. As I reached the seat of political power of the country, the coveted South Block, I realized that entry was given only to a select few.

Thankfully, they were expecting me.

After three preliminary security checks, I had to make a visitor's ID. They took away my phone, wallet and the search there reminded me of a US Airport immigration search – they literally strip search you!

Always trying to crack a wise one, I mentioned, "I have utmost respect for the man. If anyone should be worried, it should be the politicians!"

Sometimes my jokes fall flat, like this one did. Thankfully the security personnel escorting me didn't make me fall flat!

Now, a lot had been said about this man I was going to meet. I had to be thorough in my research as well. The fact that he was made Chief ahead of two senior officers was something that had raised many an eyebrow in Delhi.

Couple this with him meeting RSS Chief, Mohan Bhagwat, in full uniform in Nagpur. It only showed that this man was perhaps oriented to the right wing. He was, after all, an appointee of the Narendra Modi government.

Governments are known to pick those who will heed their requests. Well, this is normal human nature. If it is correct, it is a matter of debate. I am a big fan of independence of the pillars of democracy. However, we live in a realistic world and not a utopian one!

Which is why a lot many in our organisation were skeptical about me meeting him.

"Any of the other chiefs?"

"We are only giving more fodder to those who think we are furthering the right wing ideology."

I heard them all and sarcastically retorted, "Yes, we can choose which chief to meet, because all of them are waiting to receive a call from us, right?"

For us, anything was a step forward. Beggars can't be choosers, after all. Remember, we were a bunch of young people without surnames, mandated to work purely on merit?

As I waited in a room for my turn to come, I thought of a witty line. I have come to realize that you have only about ten seconds to make an impression. If one doesn't make an impact in that much time, you've lost the person. This rule holds true in all walks of life, whether it's a job interview or a marriage one.

I entered a large room, with a few sofas in the corner, behind which there was a signboard with the names of former Army Chiefs. The last name read Gen Bipin Rawat (Dec 2016-). There was a desk and a couple of chairs. A lot of Army memorabilia and so also a lot of space.

Standing 5 feet 6 inches tall, white hair, a slight paunch, but seemingly very fit, in full uniform was the towering yet gentle figure of Gen Rawat.

"Sir, one of my favourite movies was *Avengers*. There we see Thor and Captain America. You are our real life hero sir, it's an honour to be able to meet India's avengers."

He laughed and said, "You are good with words. Don't want to become a politician, do you?"

"My job is to build public figures, not become one. And politician? No sir, never!"

And we both laughed.

We chatted about how youth need to get rid of their anglicised mindset, especially in urban metros; how places like Kashmir needed to become more Indian and that was only possible with the youth understanding India. He immediately took a liking to what we were doing. The vision was to inject Indian-ness and my aim was to make the Armed Forces personnel heroes for school children. Something that worked well in everyone's interest.

And then, as we were about to wrap up, I asked him his views on the current government. "Not everything they want to do turns out as envisaged, but they attempt to do a lot of good."

As I expected, sympathetic to their cause.

"But, we must take the Forces to young urban people, whether it's the NCC or in some other form. We should give every young Indian an opportunity to experience the life of a soldier," he added.

I was very happy to hear this. In a country as large and diverse as ours, conscription wasn't necessarily the solution. But giving sheltered city netizens an opportunity to get disciplined was a must! After all, imagine, even if fifty percent of us young civilians had the discipline of those in the Armed Forces, the country would already be developed.

Many years later, some of this came out in the form of the Agnipath Scheme. Quite the visionary!

As I started requesting, "Sir, can I have ..."

"Yes, a picture!" he completed it.

He called his official photographer, asked me to check my hair and then the angle. I laughed. He knew all about us millennials, and more importantly, how to check all the boxes. And then asked me to see if the photographs were to my liking.

"Important picture, this one!" he said.

True indeed! The start of something which I prayed continued well beyond us... the start of celebrating Armed Forces on all days of the year, and not just on 26th January and 15th August.

He gave me a tour of his office as I prepared to leave, and then left me at the end of the corridor with the words: "All the best, young man! We're counting on you."

To be able to meet and spend so much time with the Chief of Army Staff was one thing. But to see him conduct himself with such dignity and drop me off to the end of the corridor signified something which only further got reinforced over time – he was a man of honour! Someone who treated everyone with the same respect.

Small gestures like these go a long way in showing how people perceive you. How many times do we see off those who come to meet us? Yes, the more senior ones for sure, but what about the juniors? I promised myself to see everyone off to the corridor/ car, a practice which I can proudly say I've done every single time.

Since that rendezvous, we started calling Armed Forces personnel to almost all the conferences we could. It became an unsaid norm. His office was helpful in ways more than one. I had a chance to meet him on my visits to Delhi, and he kept making fun of me.

"How's the work of making us into heroes going?"

He always dropped me off to the end of the corridor with a smile on his face. No matter how busy he was.

But for me, I always wanted to invite him to come and address the organisation in person. But somehow, due to official engagements and the border skirmishes, I.I.M.U.N. wasn't able to host him.

And then I decided to call upon him once again in early 2019. I knew that the schedules of all these very prominent luminaries get made early enough, and so I went with a letter for our Championship concourse or Annual Finale in August. Scheduled around Independence Day, this is our most coveted event of the year. In 2019, we rented out an entire city close to Mumbai, called the Aamby Valley City. This conference was one which saw the entire Advisory Board of I.I.M.U.N., Ambassadors of nations, numerous speakers from different walks of life, along with principals and students from more than a hundred cities in attendance. Think of an educational IIFA/ Oscar ceremony. A perfect opportunity to have him attend! And so I met him, along with one of our advisors.

Looking at the advisor, he spoke with a smile, "He has got you so that I can't escape and have to attend, right Rishabh?"

"Haha, yes sir. Any date between 15th-18th August, sir."

"15th I need to be in Delhi, but umm…" he was in thought.

"Sir, I need your word. You have to come this time," I insisted.

His tenure as Army Chief was going to end that year. Now this was a man of honour, known for keeping his word. So, as soon as he gave it, I was relieved. Not just because I wanted to call him as Chief Guest in front of the most distinguished luminaries at I.I.M.U.N., but more so because I had grown very fond of him and wanted to spend more time with him.

After the official confirmation, visits from the local Army station started. Aamby Valley is between Pune and Mumbai. It was decided that he would travel from Mumbai in a Helicopter and then land at the Naval Station close to the city, drive from there and then stay the night with us. A plan that was rehearsed and movement checked at least five times.

In the midst of one of our busiest conferences, I got a call from the Army HQ on 16th August 2019.

"The Chief will speak to you now."

I thought to myself, *Can't be good news, if he wants to speak to me right now.*

"I don't know what to say, Rishabh. I am really sorry. I didn't expect that I wouldn't be able to keep my word. I'm really really sorry. The Prime Minister has called for an urgent meeting and I will have to attend. I am ..."

I could sense how despondent he was. He understood the value of the occasion. He knew how much it meant to me, more so to the thousands of students who were expecting him. In the middle of everything that he was tasked with, the man recorded a video message and sent a 3 star General in his stead.

Soon, news arrived that Gen Rawat was becoming the Chairman of Chief of Staffs Committee. For ordinary folks like me, that means he would be the person who coordinates joint operations of the Armed Forces.

We got in touch with his new Staff Officer and someone who has over a time become a good friend, Capt Robin Chakravorthy. It's rare to meet people in their thirties or forties, in positions of power, especially in Indian bureaucracy. You have to wait for your turn. For me, I've always felt meritocracy is something that should be the norm. The best age that people have to give to the nation is between 25-45. What's the point if they're not utilised then?

So when I met a relatively young man from the Indian Navy who was posted with him, we bonded out of common interests in cinema, sports, and more so, poor jokes.

As I kept telling him, "Robin, when are you making me meet Batman?"

He jovially told me, "Never, if you keep cracking these one liners."

Like his boss, he understood the value proposition of I.I.M.U.N. Few in Delhi have – one of the flip sides of not publicizing your work enough.

But anyhow, just as he was about to retire, the government announced they were finally creating the position of Chief of Defense Staff – the highest ranking uniform officer on duty in the Indian Armed Forces. Chief Military Advisor to Minister of Defense and permanent Chairman of the all powerful Chief of Staffs Committee. The liaison between government and the Armed Forces. It came as no surprise that India's first Chief of Defence Staff was Gen Bipin Rawat.

I met him to congratulate him and remind him of his pending commitment. And before I could, he promptly said, "Yes Rishabh, I remember!"

Suddenly, Gen Rawat had become front page news and one of the country's most powerful people. Of course in the capacity of Army

Chief as well, he was much sought after. But now, even more so! Here, I must confess, nothing changed – neither his overall demeanour, nor his approach towards me or the organisation.

The true test is how many of us don't succumb to this notion of fame, money and power! How many of us stay true in the dark and how many of us keep our honour intact!

Robin finalised a date for February 2020 and then I guess fate had its way. The world knows what happened.

But he kept his promise of addressing us, though he did it digitally, at our Annual Championship conference in August 2020. By then, it had been almost four years since I'd first met him, and despite my personal rapport, the Core Council and the organisation were meeting him for the first time. In their nervousness, they forgot to send the link.

We sent it only twenty-four hours prior to the engagement. And on sending the zoom link, we realized that the big gremlin was that he couldn't address via Zoom.

The Central Government had asked all office bearers to refrain from using Zoom.

And for us to shift the conference to a new platform, twenty-four hours prior, was an impossible task. This couldn't be happening again.

I had to break this jinx.

I called Robin and almost broke down, "You have to do something buddy."

Gen Rawat agreed to come on Zoom, because of not wanting to inconvenience students at the last minute.

And I was very grateful.

Sometimes in life, the universe sends us angels. In this case, the angel was Robin. Watch out for these ordinarily extraordinary people; they are much more than life guards.

Making up for lost time, we followed this through with another live digital interaction in January 2021. By now, the organisation had changed its Advisory Board. We were fortunate enough to have Former Chief of Indian Army Staff who led us during the Kargil War, Gen V.P. Malik; Former Chief of Indian Air Staff, Air Chief Marshal P.V. Naik; and Former Chief of Indian Naval Staff, Admiral R.K. Dhowan – all 3 join the Board.

A particular incident involving Gen Malik comes to mind – where after a late evening program, he reached for breakfast at the allotted time of 05:00 hours. And as I arrived two minutes later, he looked at the watch and jovially chuckled, "Two minutes late, Rishabh." Military precision indeed. Well, what happened next? Find out more about this and some other incidents in #NothingButTheTruth volume 2 perhaps?

As Gen Rawat addressed the organization for the second time, all three were in attendance and were fondly looking at a man who was their junior in age and experience. Another thing I've picked up from the retired Chiefs is the ability of people to see their success in others.

Usually, when juniors/peers do better than us, the green-eyed monster of jealousy comes through. But in this case, I learnt how and why should one see it from this perspective. True success is when we succeed with others, and not alone.

As COVID was beginning to subside, I had to fulfill my long held dream and that was to ensure that Gen Rawat attended a physical I.I.M.U.N. conference. We weren't allowed to gather students in tens of thousands, though I wanted him to see the impact we could have. I was concerned about mass gatherings. Something which our politicians clearly didn't seem to be bothered about. Remember those big rallies during the pandemic?

We zeroed down on 14th November 2021 as the date.

It was Bal Diwas or Children's Day, and for a man who truly believed in youth being the future of the country, this was the perfect occasion.

And unlike the political class, which loves to pay lip service to the youth, I could see this in action.

Robin was given so much to do. He often told me that the exposure he received working with Gen Rawat was more than he would have gotten elsewhere at that time and age.

We booked the largest conference room at the World Trade Centre, Mumbai and selected a hundred students from twenty schools across the city to come together to witness the man, live. Tens of thousands joined via different digital platforms. And as the day arrived, I must admit, I was ecstatic. Not just because we were finally hosting him in person, but because this was the venue which hosted the first ever I.I.M.U.N. conference.

I was filled with nostalgia as I gave my normal speech interlaced with my self-deprecating humour and a pinch of motivation. Now, you must know this about me by now, that I enjoy talking and Robin knew this and had forewarned me.

"Gen Rawat sticks to the decided time, not a minute more, not one less," and therefore I had no option but to conclude in the designated ten minutes.

But this was the first time he saw me speak. And if you'd see me in person, I'd like to believe I'm 5 feet 10 inches, lean built, unkempt hair and ridiculously soft spoken. But give me a mic and put me on stage, and all the stage is my world! Though I don't think that's how Shakespeare envisaged it.

Even after so many years of knowing me, I don't think Gen Rawat expected such an orator. He looked at me, impressed, wondering where the sudden baritone voice was coming from.

He read out a few lines from his prepared speech and then kept his paper on the side and spoke from his heart. The topic was "Lessons from the Armed forces for leaders of tomorrow". And it came naturally to him. He received a standing ovation at the end of it.

Thereafter, I moderated a Q & A with the students.

In this segment, he really came into his own. What was most satisfying was the reaction of the audience. Students from affluent schools were all cheering:

"Jai Hind!"

"Proud to be an Indian!"

And some even said, "Bharat Mata ki Jai!"

A sight which would've been difficult to see during my school days.

Remember, you may become Sundar Pichai or Priyanka Chopra, but you will always remain an Indian first.

We then proceeded for a private interaction with principals of these schools. As they all sipped their masala tea, Gen Rawat hit the nail on the head.

"Education institutes are the second homes for these students. If the people there aren't going to be patriotic or nationalists, whichever way you see it, you will not have a changed mindset."

How many of your teachers told you stories about Indian war heroes, whether it be Bangladesh liberation war or that of Kargil?

How many of them even know about them?

He didn't mince words, and luckily, the principals resonated.

Some say there is a big push towards Indianisation in education. Some of you are studying, or have children studying in schools. You tell me, is there?

Robin gestured that we had ten minutes to go, but Gen Rawat abruptly ended, took a picture with the principals and walked towards the exit. The student volunteers hurriedly returned to their positions to form man aisles. Robin and I looked at each other, confused.

Not a minute more. Not a minute less. That was always the case with him.

But there was a reason. As he was leaving, he did something which I will take to my grave as the most wholesome life experience I've witnessed.

The man shook hands with every single last volunteer that was waiting for him.

He thanked them, took pictures with them and spoke to many of them.

Now, there was no need for this.

But he explained getting into his car, "The students are the ones you need to mould, Rishabh! Nobody else matters."

Little did I know that those would be the last words he would ever tell me.

***

8th December 2021 will go down in Indian history as one where a helicopter malfunctioned, and in the process, India lost one of its finest sons.

The government lost its first Chief of Defense Staff.

But I lost one of the few men who really cared about young people, irrespective of which background they came from.

Who cared what they wanted.

Who believed that the only way the country would change is because of the youth.

Unfortunately, the helicopter crashed with his wife and also his immediate team, including Brig Lidder, who I had corresponded with just a few days ago.

As the news flashed, it was horrific. They said Gen Rawat and the others were being taken to the hospital. They read out the names.

And in my heart of hearts, I was praying that Robin wasn't there.

And the universe was kind to me.

A few hours later, they pronounced him dead. Who would've thought that 14th November 2021 would be the last time I saw him.

It just seemed like yesterday, that he was indulging in *chai pe charcha.* And joking about how I didn't comb my hair.

That day I realised how uncertain life is. It hits you hard when someone you care about passes away. It made me understand that I must not take anything for granted. Here was a man who was hail and hearty.

Every second counts. And for a few months after that, I've never felt more alive.

As streets were decorated with posters of a real Indian hero, media cycles were fixated on this piece of news. People who didn't even know him were writing eulogies.

Luminaries from cinema, sports and politics, who had fleetingly met him once, clamoring to visit his funeral. Robin called me with an invite, and we both cried on the phone. I didn't go. I couldn't see such hypocrisy. But Robin was in service and had to attend.

Few valued the man when he was alive, but now everyone wanted a piece of him. Society.

I felt empty, because Gen Rawat was a good man.

A man of his word.

A man of integrity.

A man of honor.

He will truly, in every way, be my first Avenger.

Amen!

There are people who dedicate their life for the nation – some by serving us on the border and others by creating resources for others.

But then there is no denying that in the corridors of power as well, money talks, and those who control money determine what the country talks about!

Is too much capitalism bad for the masses? Come, let's find out how money moves.

Chapter Seven

How Money Moves

With Deepak Parekh

Growing up in a Gujarati business family with CNBC news playing on television every single day and *Economic Times, Forbes, Fortune* amongst the many business newspapers and magazines subscribed to, I grew up around buzzwords which were all synonyms of money. The world of money allured me. Not so much making money, as understanding how money works and moves. And, of course, how the rich get richer.

Therefore, it came as no surprise that I dropped science in the ninth grade and only focused on business/ commerce-based subjects.

I wasn't interested in science either, and to be honest, neither was science very interested in me.

On the other hand, I have always believed that the world of finance controls the rest of the world. I mean politics, art, cinema, sport and even science – each and every conceivable field you can think of requires currency.

Think about it!

I was one of those studious kids in school...the ones who always sit on the first bench. Read more than what was necessary, finish the textbooks before school started and would answer all the questions. A classic nerd, but one who loved pranks and challenging authority.

Someone who enjoyed asking questions beyond the syllabus, a trait most of my classmates didn't admire much.

In the world of money, I had always been fascinated by theories of how the globe was controlled by certain institutions and families. Whether it be the 'shadow people' at McKenzie or the Rockefeller and Rothschild banking behemoths – all of it intrigued me.

India is no different. Less than 1% of the population owns about 40% of the wealth. And you'll be surprised that most of these top 1% have remained in that bracket for generations.

The circles where money flows from are limited, and access to them, restricted. Whilst many unicorns think they're in control, I have come to realise they've pawns on the chessboard in the world of money.

As a young boy of 19, without a surname, approaching people in the field of business wasn't the easiest. Surprisingly, I was endearing to many of them, maybe because I was trying to do something that wasn't about me and carrying myself as if I had my life plan figured out at an age where most my age were figuring out what to do.

I won't lie. Even I didn't have everything figured out.

I was just confidently talking my way through it all.

India has had the Ambanis, Tatas, Birlas and now the Adanis. But whether it be India's Silicon Valley or the Bombay Club, everyone needs a loan. The man who is still considered the gold standard of Indian industry is a man whose uncle HT Parekh founded what has become the powerhouse behind Indian businesses. Housing Development Finance Corporation or HDFC has interests in banking, life and general insurance, asset management and venture capital. Simply put, for all those not interested in other commerce based terms, in all things finance.

Here's something that will help you put this into perspective. As of February 2023, HDFC Bank is the fifth largest private sector bank in India. By the time you are reading this, HDFC Bank would have absorbed HDFC, which is the largest private mortgage lender. Post the merger, valued at approximately USD 160 billion, HDFC Bank will be in the world's top 10 most valuable banks. Putting both India and the bank in a prodigious position on the world map of finance.

Since my early teens, I used to accompany my father to business award functions. I would see a bespectacled, studious, grey-haired gentleman with a reasonably healthy frame, at approximately 5 feet 6 inches. He would come in the same monotonous coloured suits and be a part of the jury, or always get some lifetime award. This man would inevitably be seated in the middle of the first row, next to the Chief Guest. The awards would change, the business leaders who attended would also change, and so would the guests. But this man was a constant.

I remember my father clearly telling me, "Mukesh Ambani has him on speed dial, Anand Mahindra asks him for counsel, Kumar

Birla considers him to be a doyen in the industry, and the entire stock market moves if he as much as says something!"

"Who is he, dad?" It had piqued my interest.

"Wizard of the financial world... he's the Chairman of HDFC – Deepak Parekh."

And then he added, "If you are lucky, one day you will get to meet him."

At one such award function, as I clapped for the Albus Dumbledore of Indian industry, I had decided I wanted to be his Harry Potter.

Fortunately, I grew up in a neighbourhood which housed some of India's most successful industrialists, and so I had seen them up close. But due to my introverted, socially reclusive nature, I barely ever spoke to any of them. Okay, not that I had much of a chance!

It's glamorous to say that you live in an urban precinct called South Mumbai, only to then realise that there is more VIP movement in Malabar Hill than there is in any part of the country. Considering I wasn't a VIP (Very Important Person), in fact not even an IP (Important Person), therefore for Ps (persons) like us, we were always on the receiving end of this VIP treatment.

But before I digress into first world problems, let's get back!

When I had started I.I.M.U.N., I had made a conscious effort of inviting business leaders. After tasting moderate success in inviting people from this fraternity between 2011 and 2015, I wrote to the big man.

Industrialists are a very different breed from the rest of us. Most prefer to remain out of limelight, usually focus on their work, and just like other blue blooded people, live in a world of their own. To find good reason for them to get associated has been one of my most fulfilling journeys at I.I.M.U.N.

***

It was early 2016. His executive aide called back and said, "Deepak would be happy to meet you and one of your colleagues."

My heart skipped a beat. I was uncontrollably excited to meet him, but even more so, I was elated to tell my family.

There is no bigger validation than family, isn't it?

It was time to enter Hogwarts.

Aman Baldia, a Core Council member, and I rehearsed what we were to speak to him about. We gave great thought to what we were going to wear. People say don't judge a book by its cover, but nobody ever picks up an unattractive cover. Remember, your first impression is your last one!

We didn't want to come across as a couple of college kids wearing track pants. Neither did we want to wear formals and seem like young executives looking for a job. With a shirt, cardigan and a pair of jeans, we took our chance.

I vividly recall, it was 10:45 am when we arrived at the swanky yet elegant HDFC office. IDs checked, we were taken to his floor, where we noticed many trophies, and some pictures of him playing cricket.

Like almost every Indian, Deepak Parekh was a cricketing aficionado.

Cinema and cricket unite the country like nothing else. Add these two in whatever you are doing, and you will become the cynosure of all eyes in your field.

Just as the clock turned 10.55, I was about to go and do my customary hair check. Yes, vanity is my weak point. Just then, we heard footsteps rapidly approaching us.

Almost panting, a 70+ year old man, profusely apologetic, mentioned, "Boys, I'm really sorry."

I thought in that moment that something important may have come up and he had to cancel the meeting. Kind of him to come, but he could've sent anyone to intimate us!

But he said, "I will have to take you in only at 11.10, really sorry. It's just that it's a very important business meeting which may get extended."

I was shocked. I didn't know what to say. Baldia, as I fondly call him, had the presence of mind and said, "Sure sir."

Let's analyse this for a second. Most of us don't bother reaching on time. In a city which is notorious for its reputation of being fashionably late, this man had walked outside his cabin and about 750 metres to the waiting area to apologize to two boys he was meeting for the first time. Both of whom were one-third his age.

Sure, I was fascinated about how money works. Sure, my dad was a huge fan. But this gesture had won me over.

I was to find out soon that this was only the start.

How many of us inform people when we are getting late? How many of us have made tardy excuses whenever we deviate from schedules? I certainly have!

I promised myself to honestly inform people whenever I was running late. In most cases, I've attempted to have someone accompanying me inform the person at the next meeting, but I must confess, I haven't been able to do it personally – the Deepak Parekh way.

To be honest, none of the luminaries I've met have done this either, barring some from the Armed Forces.

All I could think about as I set my hair was – what a genuinely grounded man! We weren't of any use to him and even still! Looking at myself in the mirror, I took a deep breath and promised myself not to get overwhelmed.

After all, this was the first time we were entering Dumbledore's cabin.

"My father absolutely adores you," I said to the man as I entered the spacious thousand square feet cabin. It had a long couch and a couple of one-seater sofas facing each other, and in between all this was a rectangular table. The other end had a modern wooden desk and three chairs facing a head chair, that overlooked the room. A few books, trophies, lots of newspapers and some photo frames adorned a room which had a lot of free space. Simple, but well done, befitting a man who seemed rootedly elite.

"And so you don't?" he said, chuckling to himself and gesturing towards the sofa.

"Umm, no no… Of course I do," I muttered taking a seat.

"Sir, we spent the better part of yesterday deciding what to wear," Baldia chimed in to everyone's amusement.

Saviour! I've realized, the people who've worked with me are the ones who've always been smarter than me. No wonder, all of them are doing so exceptionally well!

He offered us juices and aerated water, and I really felt like a school kid in my principal's cabin.

We had gone inside with the aim of asking him to do a session on "The impact of the global economy on India with special regards to its impact on the youth", but came out of with very different learnings.

He spoke to me in parts in Gujarati to calm my nerves, spoke about our lives and why we do what we do. He took interest in the working of the organisation and spoke about cricket. As he dropped us to the elevator, I realised why he was India's most bankable advisor.

"Remember, you are doing good for people, but don't expect anything in return," were his parting words.

Most of us do good with an expectation that something positive happens to us in return. And as much of an altruist I have wanted to be, it's been one of the toughest pieces of advice to follow.

When you add what he said to what RSS Chief Mohan Bhagwat taught me, you see it in action when it comes to people such as PT Usha. As I've grown in age and some white hair, I have realized the value of it.

A few weeks later, for the day of the rendezvous we had selected the team that worked one level below the Core Council, i.e. the

Leadership Team of the organisation, which had some members based in Mumbai. Dressed in full formals, all of us reached the HDFC premises. Now, on the same floor as his cabin is a state of the art thirty seater conference room with advanced video conferencing facilities, chairs in which you could sink comfortably and big windows. Fancy!

I have come to observe that for important people, time is currency. How much time they spend with you is how much they value you. And we were very fortunate that the man spent 120 minutes of his against the stipulated 60 minutes.

But what bowled me over was that he called everyone who was coming to meet him to share anecdotes with us. Even after two hours of talking to us, he called his economist to give insights. I've always let students take the lead in such interactions and not asked questions, as the guests are there for them and not for me. However, just as time was running out, one of the student leaders seemed to have read my mind and asked the million dollar question, "How do the rich get richer, sir?"

"You must ask those who are rich, haha! Hmm... not only do they work, but their money works for them. It's either invested in the markets, assets, or is earning interest in the bank. That's how the rich get richer."

So whether you make two thousand rupees via pocket money or earn millions, remember never to keep idle cash. Invest it, bank it, do something with it! An advice that's held me in good stead.

That day, my dad, with his strong middle class value system, couldn't stop beaming as he told every friend of his, "My son met Deepak Parekh, you know!"

Indian parents are the proudest of their children's achievements, especially when they don't expect them to do it! ;-)

Many rendezvous and years later, we invited him to the Mumbai HQ of the organisation to deliver an address to the National Leadership team. Fifty of the brightest young minds of the country, who led their respective cities from Srinagar to Tirupur, had congregated for a week-long intensive leadership camp.

Initiated in 2012, and then modelled after RSS camps, I.I.M.U.N. too has annual camps for those who are the torchbearers of the organisation.

However, in our case, the venue was a small office space which had an elevated platform and a podium at the helm. Picture a typical classroom. On the stage was the podium, two chairs and a tiny round table that barely fit. Dressed in a simple shirt and trousers, India's financial wizard entered what I'm certain is the smallest office he's been to.

We are blessed that many renowned role models have spoken at I.I.M.U.N. HQ, but no one has come with a fully documented speech. The man had prepared a speech that ran into pages and he carefully narrated each aspect that we had requested him to elaborate on.

A masterclass in finance.

The student leaders were left flabbergasted. The amount of effort he had taken for just fifty young people was nonpareil.

Thereafter, we had a Q&A moderated by me, in which he had asked me to share the questions beforehand. I was standing and asking him questions, and he insisted that after asking every question, I sit down.

"No, I'd prefer standing sir."

"No, but I'd prefer you sitting."

"Respectfully sir, how can I sit when you are standing?!"

"No, I insist."

Now, one can't argue with Deepak Parekh, so I awkwardly sat down.

He had prepared answers for all the questions I had sent him. It wasn't just a masterclass in all things money, but a masterclass in how to conduct oneself. To pay attention and respect to every small thing that we asked for showed how much respect he had for the audience.

For many, the requests of those who are below them in hierarchy aren't as important. But then again, what would we be without them?

How about being Deepak Parekh and making all of them feel included?

That's exactly what he did, by answering each and every question in the third and final segment which was interacting with the cohort. He overshot his stipulated time, but he undoubtedly became everyone's favourite speaker at I.I.M.U.N.'s Leadership Camp.

Though, for me, the highlight was an incident which I will never forget. The elevated platform was set up with the podium and chairs in a way that to try to move from behind the podium and to sit on the chair was difficult because of the space crunch. One would have to move the podium off the stage and only then be able to move to the chair. Instead of asking for help from people to move it, this gentleman was attempting to lift it off the stage himself. Two young girls carried it off, as he too continued to contribute in lifting it.

"Why should someone else do it, when I can do it myself?"

Narendra Modi talks about *aatmanirbhar* Bharat, but here was a real life example.

In a world where everyone is obsessed with VIP service, here was a man who was happy to do things for himself, even in a place where he was a guest.

I saw some of the student leaders get misty eyed.

I had built up his profile, but now they understood why he meant so much to me. It wasn't his achievements, his financial advice alone, but the person that he was.

Devacha manus aahe – as some of the Mumbaikars in the team would refer to him as.

***

It was the Thane Chapter conference of I.I.M.U.N. The students had created an elaborate set up for the Chief Minister, who had promised to attend. However, one thing I've realized is that for 99 percent of the politicians, young people are only important for optics or votes. He bailed last minute.

I am certain he had something more important that came through, but then again, sending a video message apologizing to the students and wishing them luck wasn't all that hard.

To make matters worse, there was unseasonal downpour. As it was an open aired venue, the equipment, chairs, the entire set up got drenched. It had started raining in November in Mumbai! Yes guys, climate change isn't a hoax. It is real!

The back-up Chief Guest, aka the Cheap Guest, i.e. me arrived to a cramped room with over three hundred people. There was no stage, no lights, no technical set up and perhaps barely five feet space between the first row and the podium.

An eighteen-year-old team leader along with a bunch of sixteen-year-olds had to do all the heavy lifting from the outdoor space to this indoor classroom. But as the ceremony started, she observed the podium being in a position which would make movement difficult. All eyes were on her. Instead of waiting for someone else, she looked at me sitting in the first row, smiled and started changing the position of the podium herself. As I got up from the chair to help her, she had already done the needful. I smiled.

This girl had attended Deepak Parekh's session and was a part of our Leadership Team.

His job was done.

How many times in life are we in such similar situations?

Do we get angry at the hotel staff/ house help/ office boys?

Or do we do it ourselves?

I mean, the pandemic taught us that even the most celebrated superstars were washing their own clothes and dishes, but since then, how many do it?

Why wait for another pandemic to remind us that?

I don't know about others, but I promised myself to do tasks by myself, whenever I could. And I've tried to stick to my promise.

I started with something as small as making my own bed.

Crypto currencies are the Gen Z way of multiplying money. And it came as no surprise that many of the student leaders asked him pointed questions on this. His answer, and I shall paraphrase it, was – "What isn't traceable, I cannot trust."

He was trying to mildly put across the fact that anything that makes you money overnight isn't an instrument of finance, but an instrument of gambling. Crypto currency was unregulated market and therefore to repose faith in something that was transacted majorly on the dark web wasn't sensible. It was old school wisdom to young leaders, and I must admit, there was quite the back and forth.

But he took the time to explain to them how money is printed vs how bitcoins are mined. How stock market exchanges work vs how crypto exchanges are governed. So much effort, and more importantly, almost three hours of his time.

Youth was definitely a stock he believed in.

Post the session, I saw how quickly money can be raised and it's faster than the fastest pitches I've seen in TV shows. As he sat down in our comparatively modest conference room, he made a few calls to his industrialist friends for a hospital that needed funds. In a few minutes, he had raised tens of crores. Another life lesson – Money moves because of goodwill. India Inc. trusts this man and so do I.

However, in a world which is fixated with building large wills, it doesn't matter for most whether the will is good or bad. Remember goodwill is the currency which dictates how far you'll go.

Deepak Parekh does not have the wealth that some industrialists have, but he has much more than that – goodwill.

The lesson was, focus on goodwill more than a good will.

We then spoke about politics, current affairs, our love for sushi, global markets and what not! He treats me like an inquisitive child who is always asking questions.

In the eyes of my dad, my single greatest achievement to date is to have him join the Advisory Board of I.I.M.U.N.

And every time I meet him, I realise why. It's a life lesson on how to lead life. And every single time I meet him, I take a picture.

As he walked out, he smiled and asked the student leaders how they liked the session. When was the last time your teacher asked the students if the lecture was okay?

Oxford dictionary defines humility as 'the quality of having a modest or low view of one's importance'. People say you must be humble in life, and here was the living apostle of humility! From coming out to apologize for running ten minutes late to now asking students how they enjoyed the session.

I've seen a direct correlation between success and humility. The most successful people are also those who understand the value of humility. However, in Deepak Parekh's case, analyze any anecdote from lifting the podium, to preparing a detailed speech, noting down his answers to ensuring that I sit whilst he was talking, and to helping anyone in need! You will see him as I do – a textbook of lessons in humility.

I walked him down to his car; he had come in a Toyota Camry. For a man who could own Mercedez, not just the car but the company, to be driven around in a relatively modest vehicle came as a surprise to the entire leadership team.

Today, some amongst the new rich lead extravagant lifestyles, fancy cars, big homes. Here was a man who had everything, but chose to live a simple life. Wanting good things is great, but then you'll want greater things, and then greatest things, and those will also not end. It's a cycle, and apparently, the generationally wealthy don't live by that rule.

I read a line by Gautam Buddha where he says that the problem is when you say 'I want happiness'. Remove the 'I' and the 'want', and all you'll have is happiness.

Easy to read, but quite a task to implement in today's times.

In fact, I have observed this about the top 1% of our country, especially those who are from the industry. Most of their lifestyles are very simple. They don't spend money on things they don't need. They don't buy flashy shoes and clothes with brands on them. They don't have very many materialistic desires and most lead minimalist lifestyles. They eat at the same restaurants, read a lot, travel often to keep learning, and more so, are very grounded.

They enjoy a comfortable life, but majority of them keep a low profile.

Though they may be the biggest whales in the ocean, they're very different from sharks in tanks. They allow their money to make money for them and remain generationally rich with smart investments.

Yes, there are anomalies as well. Those 0.1% who will upset the apple cart.

But a few generations here or there, goodwill dictates who remains at the top.

Deepak Parekh is undoubtedly one of the legends of the Indian industry.

To have met the man, known him and then in a small way remain a student of his has taught me a few things about how money moves, but a lot many things about how life should be led.

Whether I am his Harry Potter or Neville Longbottom, I shall let him decide. For my part, I am happy and grateful that he is my Albus Dumbledore.

It is surprising how many things in our lives are a direct result of cinema. Whether it is how movies around armed forces and their exploits instill a sense of patriotism, or whether it is Deepak Parekh's chapter ending with an analogy from the famous Harry Potter.

Come to think of it! If there is one person who is Mr Cinema himself, it is the man who many have dubbed as the King of Nepotism. A dark world controlled by few. What could I learn from him? OR what did I learn not to do from him? Turn over to find out!

Chapter Eight

Finding Your Swadharma

With Karan Johar

As Walt Disney put it, "Movies can and do have tremendous influence in shaping young lives in the realm of entertainment towards the ideals and objectives of normal adulthood."

Between a movie and a book, what appeals to you more? Considering you are reading the book, you my friend, are in the minority. Research proves that 65% of the population are visual learners; they need to see information in order to retain it. And to that end, movies are the best form of shaping minds.

The thing about them is that they are largely language and nationality agnostic. Long before Yashraj Films had made Switzerland the go-to destination for all Indians, I had the good fortune of travelling to the country.

It was the 1990s and I remember my parents speaking to locals there, who were happy to know that we came from the land of Amitabh Bachchan.

And in my most recent travels to Uruguay, I was forced to do a few romantic poses of the legend Shah Rukh Khan.

Of course, no amount of photo editing softwares could make me come close to the King of romance. But the irrefragable point is that I believe that cinema is the resplendent prism through which we can propagate our soft power.

Think of Hollywood and what they have been able to do for United States of America. Irrespective of whichever movie you pick, the villain will always be a Russian. And as a result, many people have the impression that all of them are cold-blooded and have a lot of vodka. Okay, the latter may be true, but Russians are some of the warmest people I have met.

Up until very recently, Indian cinema has been largely defined by Bollywood. The drama, the songs and the dance steps have become a part of global pop culture. And while the world knows the stars on the big screen, the people who call the 'shots' in every way are the ones behind the camera.

One of them has become a bigger star than most stars. The man who is coined by many as the 'Movie mafia' or 'The King of Nepotism' is undoubtedly the man who controls the strings of the entire industry.

Growing up in this urban sheltered precinct of South Mumbai, one was in congenial company watching Tom Cruise in *Mission Impossible* or Leonardo DiCaprio in *Titanic*.

But '*Kuchh kuchh hota hai Rahul, tum nahi samjhoge*' would only happen when one switched to Bollywood movies.

And whether *Kal Ho Na Ho,* this man was responsible for making a billion hearts beat everyday in the 90s and 2000s.

Through his Koffee show, he brought India's biggest film stars into our homes in never before avatars. And he is a constant fixture in everything that involves cinema – whether it be reality shows, award functions, hosting events, writing books and even featuring on radio shows.

Bringing to you, Rahul Yash Johar or Karan Johar! Popularly referred to as KJo, or as I would like to call him – Mr Bollywood!

Having studied at the same alma mater, I grew up listening to stories about him. And whenever I saw him on television or at functions, he was always articulate, benignant, witty and respectful towards people in general. Being unabashedly unashamed about his sexual orientation and wearing his passion for his country on his sleeve.

Now you put these qualities together. For a youth-run organisation that focusses on uniting the world, the Indian way, by sensitising tomorrow's leaders, he was a very suitable role model for the next generation.

And to be honest, during all our conferences across 220 cities, his movies had been a great way to depict Indian culture in all its complexities. In fact, we have played many of his movies as a part of the entertainment sessions for the students.

However, getting access to Karan Johar was a gargantuan task. Luckily for me, I was working on an event which commemorated fifty years of our college and it gave me access to a resource which remains my most prized possession – his contact number.

As we put together the first ever concourse of I.I.M.U.N., I messaged Karan Johar to attend an event put together by 16-22 year olds in the capacity of Chief Guest. Some of my friends, including those who had worked with him as child actors, laughed.

"You think he'll respond to an unknown message which is coming to him without a reference?" said one.

"If only celebrities altruistically wanted to do things!"

"He's Karan Johar, not our watchman Karan," added the third.

As I look back, I realise how brown-eyed and naive I was.

In my team, some prudently argued that I should go to my college principal and ask her to put in an entreaty, or ask my then girlfriend – who was related to the industry – for a favour to be introduced.

But like you would've gathered by now, I'd rather not have a person attend than taking someone's reference.

One's work should always be considered on merit, and even though it was the first year, I thought the idea was novel enough.

After all, we were teaching Indian culture by discussing current affairs in the form of debates basis material extrapolated from our scriptures. Combine this with speakers who would talk about India and intersperse this with Indian song and dance. Add a yoga session to start the day and students dressed in Indian traditionals eating Indian cuisine and how could he say no!

Of course, back then I felt the same way about Manmohan Singh, Sachin Tendulkar and Shah Rukh Khan too. Brazen presumptuousness of a teenager, but then again, the conviction with which teenagers dare to dream is nonpareil and that's what sets them apart.

But eventually, just as everyone had warned me, he didn't respond. I didn't give up. I messaged him on Facebook, or should I say the old Instagram? No response.

For someone who was inviting people for the first time, this was perplexing. I wondered what more could I do. I even went to the Dharma office every day to hand over a letter. The watchmen used to take it, but I am certain he must have thought that I was a struggling actor. Whether he gave it to Karan's team is a mystery that to date remains unsolved.

In the meantime, 2011 turned to 2013.

But I kept messaging with assiduous tenacity.

If you see my messages, I have messaged him every single year since 2011. The message has always been a few months before our annual finale. But to no avail. Then in 2018, I was speaking to a girl by the name of Palak who represented noted Bollywood actor Katrina Kaif. She was talking to someone about Karan Johar.

"Do you by any chance know who handles him?" I tcok a chance.

"Yes, Zena does!"

Now, I have realised that more than the artists, the managers themselves are a problem. Or maybe the artists have just instructed them to be like that. I don't know. But what I do know is – that without socializing and references, it's an incredibly arduous journey.

Take for example Katrina. She came all the way to Aamby Valley for our conference in 2019. She then realized that the moderator of her choice – Cyrus Broacha – had not come. So she abstrusely took ill fifteen minutes prior to entering a city which she had driven three hours to reach. In her defense, perhaps she was really sick. But no connect ever since.

One person who didn't avoid us was Zena.

I was delighted, as this was another way to get in touch with Karan. Very grateful to Katrina's team for this!

Zena put us in touch with his Public Relations (PR) team. Now these guys also had multiple layers of bureaucracy, and they too passed us on till the bottom of the food chain. But then again, I had no problem in this. Perks of being low profile.

After multiple rounds of requests being accommodated and questions being asked, we received the confirmation.

I cried out of relief! Many of the younger team members didn't understand. It was a culmination of an eight-year-long sojourn, in which time duration everything from the full form of the acronym I.I.M.U.N. to my team – everything had changed. One thing that was sempiternal was my belief system that your work should speak for itself.

However, fate had other plans.

Five days prior to the event, another lady by the name Nilufer called me and mentioned that some exigency had come up and Karan won't be able to come.

I was dolorous. We had planned everything for him – from his entry to his food – every last detail.

"Can we get him in a chopper? Private jet? Anything?"

"No no Rishabh. I am sorry, we won't be able to make it."

As I hung up, I was inconsolably despondent.

In the few weeks after that, for the first time, I felt that the universe was conspiring *against* us. We had Katrina Kaif, Karan Johar, Gen Bipin Rawat – all backing out for what was the biggest educational extravaganza for I.I.M.U.N. in 2019.

Sometimes, when you attempt with all your heart and even still things don't work out, it's a difficult place to be. In those few moments I felt I should have requested someone to assist. I questioned everything – my morals, beliefs, processes, everything.

You know the time when you think that nothing is going to work out and somehow relate to every sad song that plays? My personal life wasn't in a good place either – it was a dark phase.

But as I was watching my comfort movie, Albus Dumbledore's words kept playing in mind. "Happiness can be found in the darkest of times, if one only remembers to turn on the light."

After wallowing in some self pity and sympathy, I picked myself up. I reflected on how far we had come, how many students were impacted, how many after working at the organisation had become luminaries themselves and why we did I.I.M.U.N. in the first place. And that's how I remembered to turn on the light.

And that, my friends, is the power of cinema. I don't know which movie has that impact on you, but *Harry Potter* most certainly has that on me. So to whoever says textbooks are the best form of education, take them to the movies.

Also, in a day and age where mental health takes a regular beating, remember to switch on the light! After all, you are your best hope!

I soldiered on. But didn't receive any revert from Zena or any of the other teams.

And then in the most unexpected of places, as I was seated with my dad for the CNBC TV 18 awards show in February 2020, in a sea of industrialists, Karan Johar walked in. He had come to collect his well-deserved accolade – Entertainer of the decade.

The next day, I tried again. I wished him for winning the award. And then, as Karan Johar flashed on my screen, my heart actually skipped a beat.

"Huge apologies! I have just realized I haven't responded to any of your messages. iMessage invariably eludes me!"

As we chatted, I typed and deleted and then typed the words again to make sure I was giving my 200 percent!

"Ironic as it may sound, I would love to chat over a cup of coffee and see if joining the Advisory Board and condoning my dark humour would interest you." I messaged.

"Hey, yes sure! 3rd March."

It was *finally* happening!

That became 10th March, but that Holi is something I will never forget.

"Kehte hain agar kisi cheez ko dil se chaho...to puri kainaat use tumse milane ki koshish mein lag jaati hai."

Shah Rukh Khan said it, but I believe in it. When you really really want something, the entire universe conspires to make it happen for you!

Now, nearly ten years after I had first messaged him, I was going to meet Karan Johar. Whether or not he joined the Board, participated in the organisation's activities, it didn't matter! Just the fact that I was able to meet him was enough for me.

I hope my story serves as a reminder that consistent hard work and perseverance will get you there. You don't need a godfather or a reference or a surname. For me, this was a small personal victory.

I had to meet him alone. I wanted this to be a surprise for the students.

His security opened the door and led me into his elegant and spacious drawing room. The large windows allowed a lot of natural light that lit up the room. I stood in his living room, admiring the view in a simple white t-shirt, a pair of jeans and white sneakers.

"Rishabh, so nice to see you!" He came and gave me half a hug.

5 feet 11.5 inches tall, with a perfect jawline, hair on point, wearing a hoodie, and with radiant skin was Karan Johar himself!

I would like to believe that I am usually good with introductions, but in this instance, I was just gawking at him.

"Rishabh, are you okay? Do you want water?"

"No no, sorry sir. Just that there are very few people who I really look up to. One of them is you, so… I am just a little overwhelmed."

"Haha! Now that you are here, what will you have? Juice/ coconut water?"

"Nothing sir."

"Karan please, not sir. I am not that old."

I passed some fatuous remarks, completely contrasting my normal usual confident self. And finally, once I gathered myself, we spoke about the organisation. Why I couldn't ask for references, the Board and much more.

He politely refused the request to join the Board, as the people were too senior and knowledgeable for him.

"Amit uncle may be better suited," he said

I was confused. "Umm?"

"You don't know Mr Bachchan?!" asked a bewildered Karan.

Of course! I was sitting in the company of Karan Johar, Amitabh Bachchan was Amit uncle!

Karan had somehow managed to venture into asking me about my personal life and I had felt so comfortable that I spoke about everything, including some things which only my closest friends knew. He was great at asking a question and then patiently listening, validating what you say and making you spill all the coffee beans. The validation made you feel more comfortable.

I am no celebrity and that was not the Koffee couch. I am sure in my case he was just being polite. But what a wonderful technique! It was a masterclass in making people talk. No wonder he was such a phenomenal host. And then, when I saw the next seasons of Koffee with Karan, I saw how validation does wonders. Try this the next time you want someone to speak.

He was a great reader of people and dispensed some much needed life advice. For a person who had just met me, for the first time, I must say he was spot on. Karan was solicitous, authentic and undoubtedly benevolent.

"You are in illustrious company! Only three people iMessage me – Shah Rukh, Amit uncle and you. Rishabh, please WhatsApp me like a normal person."

We both laughed as we ended a ninety-minute rendezvous.

"I will surely attend your programs. You are contributing to nation building, so I will definitely be there to help you in any way I can, whenever you need me." Perhaps he was just being kind, I did not know.

"Thank you sir. I mean Karan. Can I have a picture?"

"Sure, but come this side! The light is better here, and wait! I'll l take the selfie."

As he adjusted the angle, he said

"3.2.1. Pout!"

And that's how I got my first picture with Karan.

I messaged him a nice paragraph on WhatsApp, to which he didn't revert for a while. That inevitably made me wonder had I said too much. After all, I have a habit of speaking more than necessary.

Don't we all sometimes analyze and overanalyze the situation? It's easy to do that in retrospect. But over a period of time, I've come to realize that what has happened should not be mulled over. Past and future are things you don't have control over. Live in the now. But then again, easier said than done.

Just as the pandemic hit, I was grateful that I had gotten a chance to meet him in time. Then was the time to check whether he would hold true to his promise. A lot of people pay lip service, but when it comes to it, they do not turn up.

I invited him for a conversation as a part of an Instagram chat show that was aimed to spread positivity.

As the day of the show neared, the organisation was looking forward to hosting Karan for the first time.

But the untimely demise of actor Sushant Singh Rajput on the very same day, led to cancelling the Instagram live.

Starting that day, Karan and most of Bollywood received such venomous hatred that would make the most sane person also lose their mind. The sensationalism of some TV channels and the desire to hold Bollywood accountable is something that has yet not dissipated.

There is no doubt that there is nepotism in Bollywood, but look at politics and carefully observe how many political families control parties and constituencies?

How many businesses, big and small, are family run?

How many people in the Armed Forces and the judiciary also have family members in the same field?

But because they were in the spotlight in the film industry, this gremlin was highlighted.

Should all fields be more democratic? Yes!

Should VIP and preferential treatment stop? Yes!

Can it stop? Yes!

Sushant's death was a tragic incident, one which cannot be condoned and the perpetrators must be brought to book! Somehow that hasn't happened yet. And that, to me, is the perplexing part.

But incessant trolling and the rise of imbecilic cancel culture must stop! It can lead to severe mental health issues, or worse. I personally know a few people who have been on the receiving end of it and it gets ugly. Moreover, before you indulge in hate mongering, ask yourself:

Would you want the same to ever happen to you?

Honestly, media trials are also quite overrated. The next time you see your friends, family or yourself getting sucked in, remember to turn the idiot box off.

Karan called. "Sorry Rishabh, can we please push it? It'll be very insensitive to do it today."

"Of course, I am sorry. I completely understand."

And this was before all the netizen trolls had began targeting them.

***

A few months later, in August 2020, I.I.M.U.N. was commemorating the start of its tenth year celebrations. As it was an online event, I didn't have much of an option, but to conduct a recorded conversation. But I wanted to invite Karan, and he was gracious enough to accept. Testimony to the fact that he would be there every single time we called him. I have seen people from his industry who have criticized him for not doing enough for the society. But what I was experiencing was different from that.

One of India's finest cultural emissaries narrated how Indian cinema has the power to break boundaries and unite people. Karan was perhaps one of the more literate voices in the industry, but what he said about theaters losing out to OTT was like Nostradamus predicting the future.

"Cinema viewing is a cultural experience in India. No one

watches a film alone; that's a very rare thing. Big ticket films, family films will make audiences travel."

And it turned out to be true. Look at Shah Rukh Khan's *Pathaan*. At the time of writing this, the Global Box office collection is over 1,000 crore. Whilst everyone was writing off theaters, the man knew what he was saying.

We had a wonderful talk and as is my habit, once it was done, I asked him for his feedback. Because I have seen how someone else's perspective can be very refreshing and eye-opening.

"You are intellectually irreverent! It's perfect for the audience you cater to, be yourself! It works, but..."

I was mentally prepared to take notes

"Work on your lighting! It's the very basic. Remember, an audience needs the basics right," he added.

The place I was taking the interview from was dimly lit. And something that has held me in good stead ever since. I haven't been big on videos and pictures, but who likes to see a conversation which isn't 'lit', in every sense of the word.

"How are things with you?" he asked me.

And a few minutes later, he signed off with, "Please let me know if I can be of any help in any way."

It wasn't just a polite observation. He was genuinely interested in helping. Someone who is deeply compassionate to people around him. I have conversed with him on numerous occasions since, and every time I speak to him, I realise that he goes out of his way to help people.

There are times when we build preconceived notions about someone, mostly on the basis of how the media paints them out to be. However, is this necessarily the accurate representation of those people? I have realised more than once that media paints a partisan image of individuals. We must be smarter than to fall prey to it so easily.

Subsequently, as COVID's intensity increased, the student interns at the organisation started compiling a database of all hospitals and centres for asymptomatic patients, or those with mild symptoms. We called this initiative – Find A Bed.

Within 72 hours, data of 448 cities was put together. However, we needed to amplify this, and who better than Mr Bollywood himself. I reached out to Karan.

"Please send me the image, Rishabh!" Just like that, he joined us in our fight to help people during COVID.

And as expected, post him becoming a cause ambassador, all cinema stars queued up to amplify the message. Now there were some who we had reached out to before Karan posted, and they hadn't reverted. But as soon as they saw his post, they messaged us.

This is something I have observed in every field. There are the trendsetters. If you win their approval, everything in that industry falls into place. Clearly shows how a few people control everything that happens around us.

Couple this with the organisation's reach in different fields, and we had thousands of people as amplifiers. What Karan did, perhaps even he didn't fully realise. He started a bandwagon impact in the most followed industry, which led to lacs of people who were able to find the website and use it to save lives. I can't thank him enough for what he did. I saw the power of compounding in action.

One person gets 3, those 3 attract 3 more, and as one of the trolls on the internet put it justly – 'Find A Bed has more celebrities endorsing it than it has beds.' Of course this wasn't the case, but I am sure you get the point.

Forbes, Vogue all covered the work of the organisation, but then again, we shied away from talking about anything but the cause. That is how with the passage of time, we stopped the publicity in every way.

"Why don't we just keep it going! Being famous helps," said one of the team members.

And then I reminded her, recalling what RSS Chief Mohan Bhagwat had said, "Our job is to make others famous, not become famous ourselves. Which is why we even used Find A Bed as the name, and not I.I.M.U.N."

Besides, like I had seen with Karan, fame is a fickle friend. He has been scrutinized more than any other individual in cinema.

But I was very grateful to Karan!

***

Jumping to 2022. Normalcy had almost been restored post the COVID waves. We had gotten the brightest and best young minds together for an annual Leadership Camp to Mumbai. Hosted at the I.I.M.U.N. HQ, the building was in a dilapidated condition and undergoing renovation.

The accepted image is that Karan won't visit such a place. His Executive Aide asked me, "Is this the place, Aman Chambers?" He also sent an image of the under construction building to confirm.

"Umm… (a rather long pause) yes!" Fearing a repeat of the fiasco that had transpired with Katrina, I was quick to add, "We can change the location, if you'd prefer."

But to my relief, he said, "No no, don't worry! We'll be there."

And there Karan was! At a run down building, which had a biscuit elevator. Most others would have their teams give us a long list of requirements. However, in his case – No hair. No make-up. No styling. Nothing.

This was perhaps a small thing, but this is what impressed me the most – the fact that he had come without any drama. And that for an industry that thrives on drama, this was a first. Yes, he knew who he was, but he knew where he was coming; this wasn't a place to indulge. I only wish others actually understood the same.

And as he sat down and engaged in colloquy with the students, he was flamboyantly unpretentious. "I want to sit on this side, my pictures are better from this angle."

The student leaders laughed.

One of his answers stuck with me. To paraphrase him:

"There's no point in faking humility, and at the same point, one needs to know one is just another human being."

I have seen big superstars fake humility and the next minute they're shouting at their staff in the vanity van. Little things matter. If you really want to know the truth, see how someone calls their staff or the waiter. I am not exaggerating or being filmi; it will tell you a lot about the person.

He was vivaciously prolific on camera, but even more so off it. As the recording stopped, I narrated how it took me a decade to get in touch with him. He was immediately apologetic, but I interjected and mentioned, "He is Karan Johar! It's bound to take time to get a response from him, but what sets him apart is how he has been since then. Always there to assist, in whichever way he can."

And to be honest, he didn't post about the interaction, nor did he carry any media. He had come solely for the student leaders and that's what he paid attention to.

At 26, he had made his debut as a director. Most people are finishing their degrees at that age, or finding their feet in the field they want to pursue. He had achieved something big, and it hadn't come easy. He cut his teeth in the business by being an Assistant Director in his early 20s. Some people might say that he was born into a film family and therefore had it easy. But this is something that you must ponder over – access may be easy, but success isn't.

What if his first few movies wouldn't have done well at the box office? What do you think people would have said?

Besides, how many of us are invested in our family run enterprises/ parents' jobs when we are at that age? Finding your *swadharma* is not an easy job, and the earlier you find it, the longer you can be at it.

I had once asked him how one could do that. 'The key to finding it," he said was, "Learn all the life skills you can, then keep experimenting till you find it!"

As we broke bread, he inquired on my plans for the future.

"You know, one of my best friends and business partners is Gujju," he told me with a smile, as he ate the dhokla.

The fact that he treated himself as just another regular guy was another charming quality.

"Keep doing what you are doing, Rishabh," he said, giving a long warm hug as he entered his car.

I must clarify, a self imposed solitudinarian, I am diabolically opposite to everyone who is a part of his 'clan'. I do not go to, nor am I invited to any soirée. So when I say this, you must believe me – this a dispassionate viewpoint on one of India's most controversial superstars.

They say never meet your heroes up close, but in this case, I am glad I did. When I had not met him, he had served as an inspiration. And now I am even more grateful that a text message turned into a long warm hug. For my part, the end of every movie is in the credits. Ending this chapter with the credit for inspiring a generation. It goes to the man, Karan Johar!

No Indian movie is complete without songs. Music has the unique ability to bridge boundaries and an astounding example of that is the standing ovation that the Oscar winning song Naatu Naatu received for the movie RRR.

But when you think of Indian music, there is one person who is – as Gen Z puts it – the G.O.A.T. The Greatest Of All Time! The magician from Madras is someone who can strike a chord with anyone. But geniuses are often eccentric. Wondering how is this man? Only one way to find out!

Chapter Nine

Striking a Chord
With A.R. Rahman

I have always believed that we are one as a human race. Yes, our nations give us our identities, but I believe in what the Vedas say: *Vasudhaiva Kutumbakam* – the world is one global village.

Unfortunately, most things divide humans, including national identities. And in a world where nation first chauvinism is the order of the day and concepts such as globalisation are scoffed upon, it is now more than ever that we need to find things that speak a common language of peace and harmony.

In this, two things bring the Ukrainians and Russians together, that bring Israelis and Palestinians, and for that matter, Indians and Pakistanis together. They are cinema and music.

No friend across the border despises a Shah Rukh Khan movie. Similarly, in my opinion, few can match the magic of Nusrat Fateh Ali Khan's voice.

And then there are some people whose work evokes global compassion.

Music has always been something that I've resorted to as an escape; one in which I can get lost for hours on end.

I am a bathroom singer and I did attempt learning the piano, but I didn't strike too many chords. Or should I say, even one! ;-)

As a child, I had witnessed the power of music first-hand. I had enjoyed the opera when I understood very little of it, or listened to a French song. The language was foreign, but I danced to the tune of it.

International music may be fun, but for me, soulful music has always been Indian music – whether it be Carnatic songs or Urdu ghazals.

Nonetheless, if someone asked me about my absolute favourite, it would be Hindi music.

I have a playlist for every occasion. My favourite singers include Shaan, Sonu Nigam and Alka Yagnik. For anyone born in the 90s or earlier, you would have definitely heard their songs, and for anyone born thereafter who haven't heard them, you must!

All that aside, I think the Magician of Music is a man whose story is as moving as his work. He was born as A.S. Dileep Kumar. His father passed away when he was only nine years of age. He was removed from school because he could not routinely attend. After all, he had to focus on earning bread for his family. Ultimately, he found his calling via music.

Sufism greatly inspired him and the family converted to Islam when he was just twenty-three years old. After initially composing jingles for various brands, his career took off in 1992, when he started composing for Mani Ratnam. And since then, there has been no looking back. Today, after 6 national awards, 2 Oscars and 2 Grammys, he is fondly known to everyone as A.R. Rahman.

Whenever one thinks about India, apart from the national anthem, there is one other song that evokes the same schmaltz and that is *Maa tujhe salam – Vande Mataram.*

The same track was played at the United Nations in New York on 13th August 2016. As we prepared for two hundred students going into what was our most prestigious concourse yet, the team and I were so fixated with getting everything right that we didn't realise what else was happening around us. A Core Council member of my team – and I think one of the strongest supporters of believing in every utopian vision of mine – Kashvi Jaggi was spearheading this project.

To unfurl the national flag on the Independence Day as the first external civil society organisation was going to be something that for us would go down in record books. But more about this in another chapter.

When I heard the song play, I looked at Kashvi and said, "Finally the Indian government recognizes the work we are doing! They're playing the song in our tribute."

"Of course! Because they don't have anyone left with white hair to recognize!" she said facetiously.

We made peace with the thought that it must be some function of the Indian government for the upcoming Independence Day.

But this girl was like the Indian Sherlock Holmes. Always inquisitive about what was happening in my life, others' lives, what happened across the country and the world! Basically interested in any canard. I'm sure we all have a friend like that.

And so she found out.

"He's coming, Rishabh!"

"Who he?"

"India's pride, the man himself, the master musician!"

"Who? Don't build it up like a Hindi K-soap opera!!"

"Okay okay. It's A.R. Rahman."

"Seriously?!"

She held my hand and took me downstairs to the main General Assembly hall and I saw the posters. I couldn't believe it! Also, this was a fortuitous happenstance indeed!

The government had pulled off an ace!

Unequivocally, one of the greatest proponents of soft power, I've always admired the panache with which Narendra Modi has flaunted Indianness.

There is no doubt that he's put us on the global map!

But was it him or some other organisation working with the government? Didn't matter! India was being celebrated.

A.R. Rahman performing on India's Independence Day would not just attract attention of the diplomatic corps or governments, but so also a lot of civil society. The focus would definitely be on India. And to do it at the UN meant the world would take notice!

Now somehow we needed to get his attention. After all, we were here for the same cause – to talk about the country and that too with the future of the nation – our youth. I am sure if we could just get ten minutes with him, we would convince him to participate in I.I.M.U.N. at some point.

And so we first attempted the official method, of asking our highest government office to the United Nations (UN) – Permanent Mission of India to the UN – for a rendezvous with Rahman. The officer laughed.

"Har kisi ko Rahman ko milna hai."

As Gen Z would say, 'True that!'

But I thought they'd be slightly considerate, cognizant of the fact that the organisation comprised of teenagers, but no!

Who cares? We've always been the audacious kinds. If we didn't get our way through, we'd find another way.

With such a big program in the offing, we were sure that he'd come for a rehearsal. And so he did. Having Kashvi by my side for this was a blessing in disguise. Now Rahman is 5 feet 5 inches and he came in with bodyguards who were 6 feet 7 inches tall and ludicrously wide! We could barely see him; getting anywhere near him was impossible. Security to the General Assembly hall was also beefed up.

By then, our Indian Sherlock somehow managed to make friends with the UN staff and enter the hall. Genius!

I waited outside as she tried to get up close to the members of his team. But to no avail. They were allowed to see him rehearse, but only from the audience. Curly haired, brown skinned and the voice of a magician- – Rahman was visible to all, but accessible to none.

When he came out, press and media were clamouring to get a piece of him, trying to force their way through the security arrangements made by the organisers. In such a crowd, we had little chance.

Now, whether you are Tom Cruise or A.R. Rahman, New York is a city where almost everyone walks. This was more because car travel there takes forever. I pulled Kashvi aside and said, "Take an intern, follow him to his hotel! The guards don't seem to be his personal security. He seems to be easygoing. Maybe sneak up to his room and speak to him?"

"What?! I will get a restraining order!" She thought I was joking. Well, it did sound like an outrageous idea.

"You are an Indian, Kashvi! What are you talking about! For the court to order anything, it's going to take forever." I said in jest

"Rishabh, you are crazy!"

I could just see the emotion in her eyes.

A.R. Rahman exited the UN. She followed him. And miraculously managed to get access to the elevator of the Waldorf Astoria. She rang the doorbell.

And that's how we first met A.R. Rahman.

He was alarmed that she had managed to track him down to the room.

But don't try these stunts; this does not normally work. And I do not recommend it.

This is the thing with the opposite gender; it mellows you down.

I did this often at I.I.M.U.N. Every time a faux pas took place, we would send someone from the other gender to apologize. Somehow your brain is geared to be nicer to them.

I don't know about others, but it's always worked with me.

As Kashvi expounded on what we do, Rahman was pleasantly astounded. What touched him was how we were spreading the idea of India. Kashvi had bettered me and invited him over to our conference. Obviously, he expressed his inability to come the next day to two functions. But he gave us his personal assistant's number and told us to keep in touch.

And to top it all off, Kashvi got a picture with him!

I was over the moon! We didn't expect this at all. But this is what I've realized – if you don't think out of the box, then you'll always be part of the crowd.

Kashvi dared to follow through on something most people wouldn't have, to follow her conviction.

Moreover, there are those who are the dreamers, and then those who are the doers. Luckily, for the dreamer in me, I had very many doers around me.

Take that leap of faith, go out there and dare to dream beyond the conventional realms of what you do. Nothing path-breaking was ever done by following the norm.

Part of Rahman's crew was one of India's most famous percu-ssionist – Sivamani. We tried the same approach with him. And it worked! Not only did he come and speak at the gathering, but he also performed for the students. And somehow generated music from the most common objects.

Now how I wish Rahman's former assistant Vijay would immediately patch us through. But the universe works in mysterious ways. We kept reaching out to his personal assistant and we were directed to his assistants. Every time we would call him from a new number, he'd say he would return our calls, but he wouldn't.

He was simply 'ghosting' us.

The issue was that he wasn't reverting. We didn't know what was happening, and it was leading to a dead end. That antagonizes me a lot.

"The coming few months are incredibly busy, perhaps 3-4 months later?"

"Next year, Rishabh!"

These are the phrases that I've learnt to live with. But to keep us in a limbo didn't go down very well with me. I am sure he didn't want to say no, or was just being polite. But if you don't want to do something, don't keep people hanging, let them know. At least they'll get clarity and chart a plan of action accordingly.

As the calendar year turned to 2018, I realized this man was perhaps not the right one. There's no sense in pursuing a dead lead. But I knew getting Rahman would mean we've maximized the field of music.

We needed to find another in-road. I knew that singers or composers don't get paid much for singing/composing songs for films. It's about concerts or the in-house creations that they hold rights over, which are the real bread and butter. He was bound to be in touch with these companies!

Qyuki was one such company that Rahman had founded with ace filmmaker Shekhar Kapur and someone by the name of Samir Bangara. Shekhar was as tough to get in touch with as Rahman, but I wrote to him. From there, I managed to get an email id where I could reach Samir. And it clicked!

Samir responded, "Let's get on a call."

"You really seem to want Rahman to get involved," was his first observation.

"Haha yes! My team member met him in 2016. He showed a lot of interest, but we've been unable to get in touch with him since."

"So how do you want him to associate?"

This was my opportunity. We had to put to best use the thirty-second elevator speech we prepare in schools and colleges. I hadn't planned it, but I pitched him the idea of A.R. Rahman joining the Advisory Board. If this happened, it would upstage getting a President to I.I.M.U.N. It would easily be the best thing to have happened in the year! Rahman was a genius and his perspective and take on issues and how to spread the idea of India would change the way we functioned. I was sure about it. And some of the best ideas that we have worked on have come from the Board.

"So, no promotions? No branding?"

"None! It's purely for the purpose of what I.I.M.U.N. is founded for – to create leaders without making noise."

"Hmm, what do you gain from it then?"

"A lot! Their ideas and when it's such an eclectic cohort of sagacious intellectuals coming together and discussing common agenda points, it's a masterclass," I said passionately and honestly.

"You are doing this for the right reasons. Let me see if I can swing Rahman on this, buddy. He loves to contribute without the Big Bang antics," he assured me.

"I will treat you … whichever place you want," I was clearly excited.

"I am a man with expensive tastes, Rishabh," he joked.

"Anything for Rahman!"

A few weeks later, he called me to his office. Bespectacled, balding, well built and fit, Samir was of average height and had a kind but serious face. He sat me down and asked me a few dozen questions. Then he called Rahman up.

"The boy I was talking to you about, Rishabh, he will talk to you now."

Covering the phone, he said, "Explain him the stuff you said in under a minute."

I did what I do best. Talk!

Then they both spoke.

He turned towards me and said, "Paperwork will follow, but happy to tell you … (this was the moment of truth) … he is on your Board!"

I got up and side hugged him. He gave me a proper hug. For someone who didn't come from a music background to be able to count Rahman as a part of our cause meant the world to me!

"Where's my treat?" Samir chuckled.

"Treats, not treat! And wherever you want them."

I have realised that sometimes doing things without seeking publicity doesn't help, but at times, it has worked to our advantage. Genuine people have been attracted to the organisation. Sometimes you cannot charm them even with lots of PR. *Do your work quietly* is a motto I have followed for the longest time.

***

The organisation had its Annual Advisory Board meeting in August 2019 at Aamby Valley City. Notice of this rendezvous was sent to all Board members well in advance. We were yet to hear from Rahman's team, and I reached out to Samir for help again. He was always very candid with me.

"Drop in an email and then we'll circle back to this in a few days' time."

The email elicited no response. Perhaps Rahman was busy. Happens to the best of us.

"I don't think he'll be able to make it. Really sorry about it," said Samir.

"Tell me what the hiccup is?" I asked him.

"Too many things on his plate and parallel commitments."

I was disappointed and understandably so. Who wouldn't want Rahman! On my next scheduled visit to Chennai, I tried to meet him. Samir mentioned he may/ may not be there, but I should talk to his daughter.

Soft spoken, a devout Muslim wearing a burqa, a young lean girl as tall as her father welcomed me to the foundations office, which was adjacent to his house.

As we spoke about instilling the idea of India in the next generation, she remarked, "Dad will love this!"

"I know, but then why hasn't he come still?"

"Rishabh, he's very busy. There's always something. Sometimes, even when he's in Chennai, he's just in the recording studio. We don't see him for days!"

We got chatting and soon became friends. She promised she'd bring it up with him as soon as she saw him.

"With no disrespect, there's no point in just adding a name, right?" I conveyed my thoughts, loud and clear.

"Yes, I understand."

According to some in my team, this was not necessary. Most were just happy having his name on the Board. But that wasn't the purpose of having him join. I had done the same thing with another very illustrious name, someone who I still greatly admire – Chess Champion Vishwanathan Anand. And much to the dismay of many in the team, he had preferred to leave.

As expected, an argument ensued within the team.

"You worked for more than four years to get him to be associated, and now you are behaving like this. Wait for sometime… he will come!"

Now the thing is that on subjects such as these, I have my ethics. Despite bearing the brunt of it in the past, I did not budge.

When the day to meet him arrived – 23rd February 2020 – I didn't inform anyone in the team. I couldn't. They wouldn't let me go. And the worst part, Samir wasn't going to be there. I was on my own.

I've rarely gone alone. I always find traveling with one more person succoring. It helps in critical junctures, like when to stop, when to emphasise on points, when I miss out on anything, and in my case, when not to crack jokes.

As I entered a simple space, I realised that as described, this was a simple man. Dressed in a nondescript blue shirt and trousers sitting on the sofa was Rahman. The living room where we met was an ordinary one – few paintings, a dining table and a couple of sofas. Powerful people make normal places powerful, and this was a classic example.

I've seen new upcoming people brazenly display opulence. And then those who have achieved almost everything. Those are the ones who wear their modesty on their sleeves. From their conduct to their belongings, everything is classy, without screaming who they are.

On a lighter note, perhaps the difference between South Delhi and South Mumbai. :-p

Rahman clearly belonged to the second category.

Thoughts crossed my mind. Should I say what I had decided? I decided to start talking from my heart.

"Sir, I know you are a very busy man, therefore I thought I'd clarify what I do and then leave it up to you."

He let me continue. And as I explained to him what we do, I emphasized on how Indian song and dance performances had been an integral part of every inaugural ceremony. That's where he interjected, "What kind of Indian music performances?"

"All kinds – from Bollywood songs to small folk music and local dance styles."

"Show me some pictures please," he asked politely.

As I juggled to pull out some images, he seemed interested.

After that, he started talking, I noticed he kept tapping his feet when he was communicating. People kept coming in to see him. But he told his team to give us more time. A fifteen-minute meeting went on for well over ninety minutes. From the role of India on the global arena, to his love for Sufi music – the range of topics was diverse.

I've observed that he kept changing subjects and was very quick with his thoughts. Whether the feet tapping was a habit to help concentration, comfort, it definitely wasn't out of boredom. Perhaps, those in the field of music can tell me why.

As he was talking, I thought, 'This man is indeed a genius! Not only did he have knowledge about multifarious subjects, but so also was fervently passionate about traditional music and Sufi songs.'

But the more he spoke, my thoughts went to all those people who would have missed their meeting with him because of me. But Rahman was unperturbed. He soldiered on. Now creative geniuses have their own eccentric quirks; not keeping time was perhaps the best out of the lot. I wasn't complaining!

And then I asked him the million dollar question.

"So what do you think? Would you be able to participate in our meetings?"

There was a dramatic pause.

"I'd love to, and even do much more. I like your honesty. You want to make a difference!"

And we ended it with taking a picture, in which I couldn't stop smiling.

I felt vindicated.

Honesty is a difficult quality to have. It's great when the desired outcome is achieved. Howbeit, when it backfires, society reminds you that one could stick to any of the 50 shades of grey. Now I understand that keeping a check on the honesty metre helps when one is speaking in public. But I still firmly believe that it's better to state nothing but the truth behind closed doors. I mean, what's the point otherwise? Try this. It'll work.

But remember, there's a no refund policy on the book. :-p Just in case.

As his daughter Khatija and I discussed, her dad was very keen to engage with us. But Rahman was unpredictable; he called one evening.

"Hi, this is AR!"

"Yes, this is RS."

"No, this is A.R. Rahman!"

"Oh, sorry sir, I didn't have your number."

"Haha, no problem."

And he went on to talk about his passion projects and what we can do.

But when I wanted to present my plan, he'd go underground and then resurface many days later.

I was grateful that I had gotten a chance to meet him before the pandemic. With the world locked up, we were engaging young people via thirty-minute long online Instagram chat shows, in which we would try to infuse positivity. Whilst the rest of my family had had enough of me, my mum – like all doting Indian mothers – diligently watched every episode.

But one episode was an anomaly. From my grandparents to distant relatives who I didn't know existed, to my neighbours and friends who had disowned me – everyone was excited to see Rahman live!

The more I read about this man, the more it came to light that he was rather reticent, but to me it didn't seem the case. He used to be doing most of the talking in our conversations. Somehow, this wasn't the case with his public interviews.

One of the journalists whose style of questioning I've always looked up to is the very controversial Karan Thapar. I remember attempting to mimic his diction in school. Even Karan mentioned that his most difficult interview wasn't the infamous one with Narendra Modi, but the one with A.R. Rahman.

"The man just wouldn't talk! He would just give answers in monosyllables. We had to do the interview 3 times over," he had said.

And surely, I was no Karan Thapar.

But then again, this wasn't meant to be a serious conversation. And in that I had a little bit of hope.

What was meant to be a thirty minute colloquy became a sixty minute conversation. He wasn't shy at all. Quite to the contrary, ARR – as he insisted we call him – was a lot of fun, warm-hearted and spoke his heart out. He even played a few songs.

The thing is – we usually stereotype people, bracket them and then decide that they're good for only those set of things. But often, if we just view them without blinkers, we kind of realise that there is much more to them than the narrow prism from which we see them.

Don't bracket people, they'll surprise you. It's happened to me more than once!

And don't let society stereotype you either! Who said a musician can't also be an intellectual who is well versed in history? For that matter, the vice versa can also be very true.

And then one day, Khatija called me.

"Samir Uncle is no more, Rishabh."

"What?! I'm so sorry!"

"Yes, he passed away in a road accident."

Samir wasn't just the common chord between ARR and me, but had become a friend. Someone who I greatly admired, both for his love of conquering unchartered territories, and more so for his unflinching commitment to mentoring nobodies like me.

It was a humongous loss. In every way.

My fondest memories of ARR are of him playing a piano and Shaan singing, as we waited for all other Board members to get together. And in that moment, I saw the Chiefs of the Armed Forces smiling, some of India's biggest industrialists, filmmakers, Boman Irani, Shiamak Davar transfixed to the music, and the best reaction was Shashi Tharoor trying to sing in Hindi! Not surprisingly, he is a mellifluous singer as well.

In that moment, I realised the power of music to unite people. If one has to strike a chord, there is no better player than the Mozart from Madras –or as he simply likes to be called – ARR!

The final chapter of the book is the one which involves multiple heartaches and setbacks, but if you have enjoyed your journey thus far, it will be your most enjoyable chapter yet.

Chapter Ten

A Broken Promise
With *Syed Akbaruddin*

When I first participated in my first Model United Nations competition in 2002, little did I know that it would go on to shape me for a few decades to come. The three-day event is one where students role play world leaders in a mock version of the United Nations (UN). They suit up and debate on international issues. Confined to less than ten urban elite schools across the country, the competitions were a phenomenon which attracted those who were equally adept in both history and public speaking. My earliest reminiscence of such a competition was where I broke down and ran out of the conference room. But over a period of time, it not only helped me overcome my fear of glossophobia (for more about this read *An Open Mic*) but also made me understand how and why we were such anglophiles.

After having won all such domestic competitions, I had a hubristic belief in my self-proclaimed genius when it came to international relations. I basically thought I was better than Shashi Tharoor.

And mind you, this was without formally having studied anything in the subject.

I had come back after one such international sojourn, where I had bagged yet another award. Presumptuously elated, basically a teenager, I went to my grandfather and told him, "I am ready to take on the family business."

Bespectacled, with a head full of jet black hair, average height and wheatish complexion, my doting grandfather chuckled. "Really! Rishabh, tell me what do you know about our family business."

"What's there to know," I riposted.

"Ok, forget business! You think you know so much about international issues, you answer me this question and you can join the business."

"Sure!" Not a bad wager, I thought.

"Why don't you tell me which was the first book on foreign policy?"

"Haha! That's easy. It was the *Art of War* by the Chinese scholar Tsung Tzu."

"Come here! That's the problem." He said catching me playfully by my ever growing dishevelled hair. "There was this guy who had long hair, but combed it appropriately. His name was Chanakya and he wrote a book called *Arthashastra*."

Two hours of a lecture later, he handed me a copy of a book that ended up in the last drawer of my book shelf.

Dada being his usual self. Who reads all this, I consoled myself.

The world is one global village. Yes, India has a few good things, but let's not go back into scriptures and mythology, etc. Besides, it wasn't cool. As Gen Z would put it, "Being a proud Indian didn't vibe as much with me."

It was 8th November 2010, and the most talked about man in the world was coming to India. The first African American President of the United States of America had come on his first state visit. For someone who was an ardent follower of current affairs, this man was – as in today's language – a G.O.A.T! Greatest Of All Time.

His charisma, prowess in public speaking and his political adroitness made him a statesman par excellence. After meeting the Indian Prime Minister, industrialists and other celebrated people, Obama – who still remains the strongest advocate of youth – chose to interact with a few hundred students at St Xavier's College in Mumbai.

All the smartest kids of the country got selected, and so did one oversmart SoBo teenager!

Obama shook our hands and called some of us by name.

"Rishabh...it is nice to meet you."

That was it. My existence had been validated.

In his speech, he spoke about how the world had so much to learn from India. And I thought this somehow echoed what my granddad had told me. An impossible coincidence.

We often listen to our role models more than our own family, don't we? A technique we have successfully used in I.I.M.U.N. When your heroes come and talk about India, you will automatically listen.

And that's why we request so many of these luminaries to come in and speak to impressionable young adults.

I started reading the *Arthashastra* for the first time. I was pleasantly discombobulated; it was the *Art of War* and much much more. I picked up the *Charaka Samhita* and whenever I re-read it, I have realised that all our mental health issues would evanesce only if this was made part of psychology curriculum. Not proud to say, but I picked up the *Mahabharata* and *Ramayana* when I was 19, and only thereafter the Vedas and a few other scriptures.

But I am glad I did.

"Money will come Rishabh, learn more about our country and teach benighted adolescents such as yourself first."

I knew Model United Nations well, but I thought it was making us anglicized, wearing western formals, simulating either UN councils or the House of Congress/ House of Lords. So we Indianised it – from simulating Indian committees to wearing Indian clothes, from eating Indian food to practicing yoga. And that's how in the year 2011, Indian International Model United Nations was born. An organisation which has gone on to spread this concept in more than two hundred cities across the country. How I only wish we had changed the full form of acronym to India's International Movement to Unite Nations before we began itself.

But getting back to our annual finale conferences, we had rented out a trade centre, a 5 star hotel and even a city. For a bunch of overenthusiastic hyperactive youngsters, the team was looking at me with bated breath as I made the announcement. For every person who has been a fervent follower of religion – for instance, if you are a Muslim, your holy pilgrimage would be to Mecca, for a Christian to the Vatican and for a Hindu, the choices are many. The same way, for every enthusiast of MUN, the nadir was reaching the coveted United Nations.

We had worked on this project for many a year, liaising with the External Affairs ministry who had put us in touch with the Permanent Mission of India to the UN (PMI). This was the apex government body to the United Nations, and all communications would be routed via them.

But, we were prepared to put in the hard yards around the layers of bureaucracy. No amount of trips and paperwork to Delhi and New York could deter us.

The cause we had selected was reforming the UN and pushing for India's seat in the Security Council. Something that the Prime Minister was a strong believer in as well.

As I announced in August 2015 – The first external youth-run civil society organization to do a full-fledged MUN conference in the United Nations wouldn't be USA, UK, French, Chinese or Russian organisation, but an Indian one" – the room erupted! I remember that speech receiving four standing ovations.

We were going to unfurl the Indian flag in the UN in front of the rest of world on Independence Day.

A proud moment. Things like that put you on top of the world, don't they?

And before the eggs had hatched, we had counted them. Of course, you can imagine our excitement at being granted permission, even if it was just verbally. But I later realised that it's better to get everything in place and only then talk about it.

Remember this – it will hold you in good stead. Whether it be the boy you are dating or the business deal you are making; make it public only when it is 100 percent certain.

Now all our conferences were three-day events, and we had therefore put in a requisition for getting a conference room for all the days.

On one of our trips to New Delhi, we were asked, "So who will be the teacher or adult coming with you?"

"No one! We are the organisers. Teachers will accompany the students who participate," we responded.

"So, you kids are going to organise this?"

"Yes, we kids."

"Which is the travel company you have taken?"

"We are the travel company."

The bureaucrat laughed.

"The Indian government has never sanctioned something like this and you do know how much of a backlash we will receive if something goes wrong out there? I can't sanction this; come back with a better plan!"

Now this is the exasperating part about most people in our country, you see a young person without white hair, most will impetuously assume that the person is a novice.

We had the plan, the details, everything in place. We didn't need their finances; we just needed their offices to forward communication. We wrote to his seniors in Delhi. No answer.

Howbeit, a serendipitous encounter with his senior in the elevator and we were able to get in touch with someone who understood how this could be beneficial for everyone.

"This will work incredibly well for the country. Young people on their own going to the UN to raise our matter in regards to the Security Council. You are showcasing to the world what India has to offer, Modi ji would love this!" said the empathetic senior.

"Sir, but the problem is, I don't think the message is reaching Modi ji in the first place!"

"Let me see what I can do."

And just like that, we were granted permission for one room for one day. But we needed it for three days. No amount of supplication helped.

"Only this much, Rishabh! Nothing more at this moment," I was told.

And so, for the remaining days, as Gen Z puts it, the team said, "We'll wing it."

Of course, we couldn't 'wing' a trip to the United States of America!

The most gratifying part of any event for me has always been the late nights, the meticulous detailing of every aspect (I have quite the OCD about it), and the endless run throughs that we do. Now ask any of my teams and they may not concur that this was their favourite part. But all of us were in consensus that this was perhaps the single most important concourse in the brief history of I.I.M.U.N.

And the intoxicating part was that it was a first for everyone involved, including the Indian government. However, I must explicitly clarify that everything from taking the students from India, booking their tickets, choosing their hotels, organising meals, taking them into the UN, procuring rooms on the remaining two days and even conducting the program for all three days was all done by a young team spearheaded by the conscientious twenty-one-year-old Kashvi Jaggi.

As the D-day arrived, I was ecstatic. It was a dream come for so many of us!

Then Senior Vice President of the World Bank – Kaushik Basu – addressed the students in the capacity of Chief Guest. But what was the highlight was unfurling the Indian flag on I-Day. As diplomats and officials from various nations stood for the National Anthem, a chill ran down my spine. It was India's time now!

"You have made us proud, and you have done this at such a young age!"

I corrected the principal and pointed at Kashvi. "She's the one you must thank."

People often forget those behind the scene. They're the real superheroes. It's easy to stand on stage and take the spotlight, but ask any performing artist and they will tell you how important the paraphernalia is. Remember to thank the ones who put you up there, who make your team. You are only as good as them. Many years later, the UN recognized I.I.M.U.N.'s work in bringing about actionable change. I chose to take a step back and Kashvi was the one making the presentation at the UN HQ, New York.

"Thank you for letting me do this," she said as if beholden to the organisation.

Little did she know that she was the reason why we were there in the first place. I don't know much about stocks, but young people are your biggest assets. Invest in them, and you'll see maximum dividends.

Now, Syed Akbaruddin, an acclaimed diplomat was occupying the senior most-position of India's Permanent Representative to the United Nations. This is a very coveted position in Foreign Service as the Ambassador deals with 193 countries.

Curly haired, sharp features, brown skinned, lean body type and standing almost at six feet tall, he was a man who was intellectually intimidating. Another thing I noticed about him which I had seen was that he didn't smile much. Or perhaps this was just the case with my jokes and me.

As the final day of the event arrived, the Permanent Mission of India had issued us passes to take the students to one of the committee rooms that are used in the UN. We were to discuss 'Reforming the UN' and the committee was going to be chaired for a while by Syed Akbaruddin.

My raison d'etre was to ensure that he likes the proceedings. After all, this was the stepping stone to increasing the intensity and scale at which we demanded a reformed UN. Not only is this a dire necessity for an outdated power structure, but also to the best of my understanding, fits well with our foreign policy endeavours.

Then, in the closing ceremony, following my address, he gave his. He was very courteous and spoke glowingly about the organisation. Afterwards, there was a Q&A with the students.

One of them asked him, "Sir, will we ever get a permanent seat in the Security Council?"

He was confident and mentioned that if civil society continues to put pressure, then things would move, else the UN itself will lose relevance.

In my humble opinion, the parlous state of the UN aside, it is fast losing the little credibility it has left.

"But can we do something to help?"

"Increase awareness about this, get a petition that young people sign and have it signed from more than ten thousand people, and bring it to me. We'll give it to the PM and also to the UN Secretary General."

I interrupted. "Sir, I.I.M.U.N. can get more than a lakh people's signatures. However, you have to help us with the UN General Assembly room, so that next time, we can carry out our three-day conference there."

"It's a deal!" said Akbaruddin, smiling at me as he received thunderous applause.

For us to be able to organise something in the very place where the Heads of Nations sat to discuss how to reform the UN and then provide them an ingenious solution would be a ginormous contribution for a youth-run organisation.

The date was finalised as 15th August 2017, but work immediately started the day I landed in Mumbai. We had planned with the PMI that we would bring artistes of international repute to perform as well. Rahman may have been difficult to get, but others would perhaps have been possible. To be honest, a lot of them had shown interest. I wanted to transcend my commitments and it would most definitely require an entire year.

Sedulously, we made this the central focus of the organisation. From Andaman to Ahmedabad and from Srinagar to Salem, any conference that was organised had the theme – "Reforming the UN: Getting India a permanent seat in the security council".

We had to spread civic awareness, so we involved local media outlets in our capacity. If one were to type 'India permanent seat in UNSC iimun" you'll get articles that run into pages. The idea was unambiguous and the strategy coherent – get maximum signatures and physically collect all these forms.

I have always seen an *andolan,* or as some would call it a march/ protest catching public attention. Think of Anna Hazare's demonstration against corruption or the great Dandi March by Mahatma Gandhi. Inspired by these people, we had taken out large walks from January 2016 and continued it with great intensity till August 2017. From blocking Haji Ali in Mumbai to walking around the City Palace in Jaipur. August 2016-17 saw over 50 marches with over 100,000 students participating in them.

Add the word 'march' to your last keyword search and you'll be surprised with the results. We felt we were a part of a big puzzle; a small part, but a part indeed. And we intended to do our best.

Remember, you invigorate young people enough, we'll believe just about anything and make the impossible happen. No wonder all revolutions are caused by the youth!

As we were going to organise the concourse in the United Nations General Assembly hall, we had to gather more students who would be willing to participate. The first endeavour had about 200; here we needed to get five times that number. The entire organisation's Core Council worked on this project for more than three hundred days.

By December 2016, we had gathered more than a lakh petitions. I animatedly communicated to the Permanent Mission of India (PMI) about the accomplishment. I mentioned how preparations were in full swing.

With much to do, I requested my proficient deputy to take over communications with the PMI. Hardik Jain always wanted to be the smartest guy in the room and he strived to achieve that. He was a student who passed engineering by studying a night prior to his papers, skimmed through law because he found it interesting and is a successful media entrepreneur today. Having worked with me for over seven years, we expostulated on every piddling matter, but he was by far one of the most trusted lieutenant of the organisation.

Hardik often used to tell me how the PMI was being derisive towards the organisation and the student leaders. And how they weren't confirming which rooms we would be using – would it be the General Assembly on all days or different rooms. I kept telling him, give them time; they have a multitude of issues to look at and we are just one project for them.

But then, December 2016 became April 2017 and the rest of the Core Council started getting perturbed. And rightly so. That's when I called the PMI.

"Please advise us on the situation."

"We may not be able to help you," responded Enaam Gambhir, a young officer.

Shocked, I responded, "What do you mean?"

"Means we cannot host I.I.M.U.N. at the UN this year," she responded tersely.

"Are you aware of the timeline? People have made bookings, taken visas, we've gathered over one lakh petitions! How can you not help!"

Radio silence.

"And why can't you help out?" I added.

"I am not at the liberty of disclosing that, but we can't help you."

"Respectfully ma'am, the PMI or the government don't have to pay a single rupee. You have to simply 'help' us get a room!"

"I have a meeting now," she hurriedly said and hung up.

I have never met this lady and I don't know the reason for such contemptuous behaviour. I know that people like to show their sphere of influence when they can, especially those in the bureaucracy, but to talk like this was ludicrous!

"See, I told you!" chimed in Hardik.

I called the UN PMI landline and requested to be connected to any senior.

Nothing happened.

I had met a few people there. I called one of them.

"What happened?" I desperately wanted to know the reason.

"Rishabh, I don't know why they've done this. You should write to the Ambassador," he suggested.

And so I wrote a letter requesting for an explanation for this inexplicable decision. Hundreds, if not thousands of students had worked to get the petitions, spent sleepless days and then not to be spoken to wasn't correct.

Syed Akbaruddin refused to come on the line. If someone were to check our communications written and the call logs, we would have perhaps set a Guinness world record of calling one office in one month.

Lack of communication isn't good.

Being imperious isn't either.

Even if you want to give bad news to someone, be polite and talk.

I learnt how not to behave from these PMI officials.

I remember my entire Core Council intermittently sleeping and eating only a few meals as we spent about a week thinking what to do.

I sought a meeting with MJ Akbar, the then Minister of External Affairs and some other officials in New Delhi.

Requesting to get on a call with someone who was behaving in such a high-handed manner was not going to be possible. I too had read Kautilya's *Arthashastra*. We had to save the reputation, and finances of an organisation whose average age was 19. I rushed to Delhi.

Before becoming a minister, he had attended an I.I.M.U.N. event in Delhi. But this time, his staff officer entered the rest room and stopped me from urinating as Priyank and I were rushed into his cabin.

"I was waiting for you guys!" he said animatedly

"Sir, I was..."

"Anyway, tell me, what can I do for you?"

As I stood and was explaining the situation, he stopped me. "I cannot help you. Thank you." He said and rang the buzzer to ask his staff officer to escort us outside.

Perhaps, he was genuinely busy, or had coordinated this response already.

The meeting lasted less than two minutes.

Even Maggi needs more time to be cooked.

We met other officers we knew in Delhi, but to no avail. We even sent our team in New York to visit the PMI, but we got the same response that we were given over the phonecall.

"There are hundreds of youth organisations. Why should we help you?"

Okay, we were nobodies. Yes, hundreds and thousands of youth organizations should press for spreading India's message in various countries. But I.I.M.U.N. had been doing it without any government support for several years. And forget all this, you should help because *you* had promised!

The one thing I learnt that day was never to make a promise you cannot keep. You don't know what it could do to the other person. In our case, I can safely assure you that all of us were going through unparalleled trauma. Our mental health was at its lowest. Perhaps my worst few days in the last twelve years of the organisation.

It was the one day where I wanted to enter politics, start a party and change the system. I have realised over a period of time why it is better to do this from the outside.

Nothing was working. All doors were shut.

I even broke my rule of not asking for a reference or help.

I spoke to Sunil Deshpande of the RSS and requested him to intervene, or maybe ask Mohan Bhagwat to do so.

"Hum kuch nahi kar sakte. Yeh Bharat ke bahar hain. Aap kaan dusri oar se pakadiye!" They were clear that they won't be able to help since the matter was out of India.

Despite being redirected to individuals who paid no attention to us in Foreign Service, I told them how students from more than twenty countries were coming and how this would dent our country's image. More so, how it would break everyone's morale.

But despite being well-intentioned, no one from the most powerful organisation in the country did anything. Or at least did anything that I know of.

It was May 2017. Hardik wrote an email to then External Affairs Minister Sushma Swaraj, keeping all of us in loop. And I followed it up with my final Brahmastra – writing to Hon Prime Minister, a man who I knew was keen on the cause and the youth.

This was all we had.

We even tried to open a back channel. Former Indian Ambassador to the UN, Amb Prakash Shah – who serves on our Board – was someone under whom Syed Akbaruddin had worked.

"Rishabh, he is irritated because you reached out to Nagpur and Delhi," I was told.

"Sir, that's because they said no to us, without any reason," I explained.

"I understand your point of view, but he's said now, let them use pressure!"

That day Prakash Shah taught me a very important lesson. Never trouble people in the middle and lower end of the food chain; they are the ones implementing the instructions. Imagine being great friends with the owner of the restaurant, but he's never going to prepare your food; that will be done by the chefs. And that is a lesson that has held me well over the years, I am now friends with all chefs wherever I go. ;-p

Coincidentally, my parents were in America in the months leading up to the event, and I requested them to travel to the PMI.

"Your son and his team have caused us a lot of problems. We had to travel to Delhi, had multiple calls and correspondences," said a harrowed officer.

But even to my parents, they were condescending. And that's where I realized that the problem was a systemic one.

In their internal response, they came out with an explanation that the UN had stopped giving its rooms for such events. And the ironic part is that people in the UN itself went on record and told us this wasn't true. Other countries encouraged civil society organisations to do the same thing as we did, and many were organised in 2017 and years to come.

But they were the boots on the ground.

Why would Delhi and Nagpur listen to us?

Why would they go out of their way to upset the bureaucrats? And that too for a youth run organization.

I am glad that whether it was writing to Late Sushma Swaraj or Narendra Modi or the RSS, at least an inquiry was conducted.

Also, I don't blame them. They have a country to run. But then, don't make tall claims that you stand up for the youth.

They do that when it's convenient for them.

I have learnt to never believe most politicians and bureaucrats from that day onwards.

No amount of obsecration or directing anger helped. The students had spent close to ten crores.

"We still have a month to go, guys," said Kashvi.

Everyone was traumatized; no one could or was willing to help us. And that's when leadership is most challenging. But after the talk, Kashvi remembered what she had heard me tell her in regards to A.R. Rahman – if you can't get to speak to him normally, go directly to his room. After all Sunil Deshpande had also said the same thing – if you can't hold your ear with one hand, then use the other one. Kashvi knew it.

What do we when every door has shut? Well, simple! We tell the universe to open another one.

"Why can't we do it via the UN?" she mentioned.

"Because it's an association of countries," added another boy.

"No, we must at least try!"

A few hours later, she put me on the phone with someone from the UN staff. I explained the situation with the same solemnness with which I had spoken in Delhi.

Here, we had a way out. We basically had a conference room for a day inside the UN. If PMI could not assist us didn't mean the UN was padlocked. Where there is a will, there is a way. And most importantly, irrespective of whoever tells you no, some diplomats told Kashvi and Hardik that they can't do anything, berated and ill treated them by stating, "they were good for nothing children". Remember, you've not lost till you accept defeat.

As we celebrated another Independence Day at the UN, it was a moment I will never forget.

I would like to believe that Syed Akbaruddin, Enaam Gambhir, MJ Akbar or any of the other officials at the PMI aren't intrinsically bad human beings. I have realised that situations make people thus and perhaps some tersely worded emails may have aggravated them further to act with unprecedented vengeance.

To date, they remain bitter about their dealings with I.I.M.U.N. and in whichever official communique we have sent to participate in any of the programs of the PMI – which as per Akbaruddin's initial email "they would love to have us join", we have been regularly blocked or not responded to.

I felt that an opportunity was missed, an exercise that could have helped India in its official capacity was relegated to another youth-led activity. Some of the signed petitions still lie in the I.I.M.U.N. office.

Ego is something that I have coined as everlasting gory overconfidence, and I have seen it ruin things. Relationships, deals and even a country's image. I learnt that it is easier to preach and difficult to let go. And for my part, to any of the individuals mentioned in the chapter, if you are reading it – I reiterate – I am sorry.

This broken promise may have temporarily fractured the enthusiasm of my Core Council, but Gen Z and millennials are more pertinacious than I am. A girl who failed in her engineering papers because of the vexatious experience, then went on to study at one of the more prestigious schools in the United States of America. And after finishing her stint at New York University, she worked at the United Nations – with an aim of bringing about change from within. And as she grew in experience, she realised the real power of the UN lies with USA, and is now working with the government there. Don't be surprised if in a decade or so, you hear of an another Indian American rising up the political ladder in Washington.

'The good for nothing boy' Hardik has a successful media empire and has opened multiple companies grossing revenues that will put some sharks in tanks to shame. Now he uses social media and his clients to spread the message and idea of India.

Young people will remember. They will bring about a change. And in that lies our country's greatest hope to unite the world, the Indian way.

My purpose behind penning this book is to serve a reminder to people that conversations with people can teach you as much as books can. Perhaps much more. Ironic that I must use a book to communicate this point.

Life experiences are like your hands. Look at them. Both hands in themselves serve a different purpose. The next time you sit down for a meal, try using both the fork and knife with one hand. It's incredibly difficult to eat food like that.

But use both your hands – one for the fork and the other for the knife – and see the seamless manner in which you can eat. Life is much like that. Use both your hands.

Your experiences will shape you and make you who you are. But one must allow these experiences to happen.

However, in our country, most of us eat with our hands, getting into a place where people use cutlery was a herculean task. And as I navigated these different fields with novel approaches – which failed many a time before succeeding – I pray that these gave you insights on how best to reach out to people. After all, network is net worth.

With these shared experiences of leadership and life lessons from some of India's most powerful people, I do hope that via my learnings from behind closed doors, your journey will be slightly smoother than mine.

As Socrates said,

"Smart people learn from everything and everyone,

Average people learn from their experiences,

Stupid people already have all the answers."

I used to be in the third category, fell into the second category because of my team, but I am certain you smart people who fall into the first, would have learnt a lot.

Until we meet in person...! Shutting the doors for now!

Backward

Backward

To be frank, I'm little depressed. When Rishabh called me up to write about his book, I rightfully presumed, he wanted me to write the 'Forward'. I mean, I have all the right credentials. I love the world of politics. I know how to spell 'Mahagath Bandaan', and most importantly, I live nearby.

Imagine the colossal shock when he said, I didn't make the forward, but that he just needed a line here or there as he was a page short. After giving this much thought, and swallowing my ego, as Rishabh is a lovely man, (he once offered 10 rupees to a beggar, and unlike me, didn't ask for 5 rupees change back), I've decided to write this for him anyway. It's just that I'd like to call my piece something. Since I didn't get to pen the forward, I'll call this, 'The Backward'.

The 'Backward'.

The book is titled *Nothing But The Truth*. In order to honour this sentiment, let me honestly say, when Rishabh sent the book to me, it did not have a cover. I hope to God, by the time you read this, the cover has appeared, otherwise, what will you judge the book by na?

Many years ago, Plutarch – of whom I'm told Rishabh is a direct descendant – gave the world his monumental writing 'Parallel Lives'. Rishabh seems to have garnered a little inspiration from his celebrated ancestor. (Plutarch descendants landed in Surat after losing a bet, and you can do the math, from there). While this book doesn't deal with duos, it does deal with interesting people from whom one may draw inspiration, directly or indirectly.

The author has that chameleon-like charm to deal with Mohan Bhagwat on the one hand and with Karan Johar on the other. Here I speak of Rishabh. To the best of my knowledge, Plutarch has no recorded interview with either Mohan Bhagwat or Karan Johar. Politically, it's fair to say that Rishabh is a 'centrist', never quite fitting in either right or left. This is a position he may have borrowed from me, and now seems unwilling to return.

We Indians are champions of the periphery, the background. Rishabh stands alone in his ability to glean specific, insightful moments from his 'stars', without cluttering his own and our minds with an overall, holistic sort of judgement call. As he told me the other day in chaste Gujarati, 'No man is perfect, but there are perfect moments in most men'.

The book though does contain one tiny error. At one point he refers to Dr Shashi Tharoor, as inarguably, India's greatest speaker. Well clearly, Rishabh has not met my wife. Yet, this is a small matter, as in a sometimes matter of fact, sometimes self-deprecating, but always engaging way, Rishabh Shah, or R.S.S. (as his initials go), brings alive some of India's movers and shakers from across a wide spectrum.

By now you have guessed, I don't have too many friends. Unfortunately for Rishabh, I count him amongst that small group. Lastly, I'll say this, no one makes more fun of India than the author, and yet no one I've met has ever loved India more. This means, one day I'll have to write a similar book myself, and Rishabh Shah will be Chapter I.

My Backward is now complete. If it sounds too much like a Forward, kindly blame Rishabh bhai. Oh, and more kindly, please buy the book.

Cyrus Broacha
C.E.O (Chief Entertainment Officer)
Rishabh Shah & Sons.